PATTI DOBROWOLS[...]

DRAWING SOLUTIONS

HOW VISUAL
GOAL SETTING
WILL
CHANGE YOUR LIFE

ISBN: 978-0-9839856-0-0
 Library of Congress Control Number: 2011961355
Copyright information available upon request.

Interior design: J. L. Saloff
Cover design: Scott Ward
Typography: Calisto MT, Creative Genius

v. 1.0
First Edition, 2012
Printed on acid-free paper.

To Lois and Joe,
who taught me that anything is possible
once you can sing and enact the entire musical,
The Music Man.

Matt & Tommy
May everydream
you ever draw come to
be in full living color.

[signature]

CONTENTS

PART TWO:
The Mapping Process: Current Reality Becomes Desired New Reality

PART THREE:
Working with Visual Maps: What to Expect Along the Way

PART FOUR:
A Quick Guide to Mapping

INTRODUCTION

If it is true that one of the only things we can count on in life is change, then knowing how to deal with and navigate changes when they happen is critical for success, happiness and ultimately, survival.

This book is for anyone face to face with a situation that requires them to make changes. It doesn't matter if the change you are dealing with is huge, terrifying and unexpected such as unemployment or a health crisis. Or change that starts with the growing awareness that something is missing in your life until it becomes a longing for something new, like more creative work or a satisfying relationship.

If this sounds like you, and you feel at a loss about what to do *right now* to navigate the challenges you're facing, this book can be your guide. Using simple, proven techniques you can transform what you wish were happening into a solid map toward the life you desire.

This technique is based on the simple truth that when you draw a picture of something you want to see happen, your brain sends out signals that begin to magnetize the results you long for. Almost immediately, you will begin to transform your life.

Let me be your coach as I share with you what I have learned about drawing solutions to your problems after years of working with individuals and groups all over the world. Go get a pen and some paper and let me show you how to draw your way out of the box you're in right now.

One sunny California afternoon I found myself on my hands and knees crying in a stranger's garden. At first I was crying because I had tried, unsuccessfully, to prune a lemon tree. The hacked-up tree showed quite clearly that I was just pretending to be a gardener, because this was the only job I had been able to find when I fled my life in Seattle for the anonymity of San Francisco.

Up until then I had been a successful actor and writer who had performed for years. My career had even taken me to Broadway. I had grown accustomed to the life I had created for myself; the fame and approval were sweet. And then something happened that I never expected: someone wrote a really negative review of my work, and me. Their words splayed across the cover of the Arts and Entertainment section, "Can't sing, can't dance, can't act, can't write, don't bother!" struck me to my core. I was paralyzed for a while and then I found I could not bear to act again. Some part of me knew that the review signaled that this part of my life was over. So, I decided to escape.

In Seattle, I was an actor who could no longer stand to act. By packing up and moving to San Francisco, I had transformed myself into a simple gardener, with dubious pruning skills. In my new life, I only needed to weed, water and prune to prove my self-worth. Here in this garden, there wasn't a soul to ask when my new show was opening.

But now, as I sobbed in the shade of the mutilated lemon tree, I realized that not only was I a lousy actor, I was also a very bad gardener. In fact, at that moment, it seemed pretty clear to me that I was a failure at everything I tried to do. Why had my life taken such a turn for the worse?

In my despair, I shook my fist at the big "up there." I think I even yelled, "Answer me! Look at this half-chopped lemon tree!" I flopped on the ground. Moments later, I heard quite clearly a crabby little voice inside my head, "Pity, party, wah! In two years this won't even matter, so get up, go call your boss and tell her about the tree. Just get it over with so we can move on." With that I got up, wiped my snotty nose, brushed off my pants and got out my cell phone.

What I didn't know at that moment was that I was entering a ten-year cycle of profound changes that would eventually find me traveling widely, leading workshops, lecturing and working with some of the most innovative people in the world.

This book is for any of you who are standing right now under a botched lemon tree of your own, wondering what will become of you. In this place of pure panic you have no idea what your next step is or how you'll ever get there. Yet you know deep inside that something has to shift, something has to change, but you have no idea how to make change happen.

Just by being alive, each of us comes to these crossroads where internally we begin to feel uncomfortable with our current state and know that something needs to shift: we

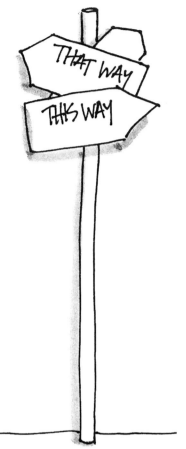

want to get healthier, find better relationships, or move to a different, sunnier climate. Sometimes the change happens suddenly. Something happens and the life we thought we had is over: we lose a job, get diagnosed with a life-threatening illness, or a loved one suddenly transitions out of this world. Whatever the initial cause, a seed is planted and our lives begin to grow in a new direction.

Andy Grove, co-founder of Intel Corporation, calls this "the point of inflection," or the seed of infinite possibilities. When we experience and acknowledge the desire to shift from where we are to where we could be, we create the possibility that we can step into a mysterious, magical and alchemical process of change that will, eventually, transport us into something new, as scary as it may seem. Along the way, we discover new parts of ourselves as we link to our own internal maps and road signs, and encounter people and places that will help us achieve the goal germinated by our desires.

While some of you may be new at this, many may already be used to navigating life changes. Change is stressful, challenging, and inevitable. If you are uncertain about your ability to change with grace and flexibility, know that you have been using your ability to adapt since the day you were born. Now is the time to take hold of your hard-won adaptability skills, and learn to literally draw solutions to help you make change more easily. This book will show you how.

HOW TO USE THIS BOOK

This book is set up so you can maximize your brain's capacity to absorb and retain information as easily as possible. It is structured in a way that will help you grasp the value of visuals, and includes drawings throughout to help you remember the concepts. While the book is structured in four sections, I encourage you to move around to find those things that you need *right now*. All roads lead to Rome, so find the route that's right for you to get there.

Here's how the book is organized: **Part One: Why Mapping Works: Visual Images and Change** will provide you with context setting and help you understand (or remember) how the brain works and why visuals are an important part of goal-setting success. It will give you a solid foundation for the process you are about to enter into. **Part Two: The Mapping Process: Current Reality Becomes Desired New Reality** introduces you to a simple visual process you will use to successfully make change happen, called "The Snapshot of the Big Picture™." This is the heart of the book and will thoroughly guide you through each step, planning and making the changes you desire. **Part Three: Working with Visual Maps: What to Expect Along the Way** shows you how to maximize the benefits of the Snapshot of the Big Picture Map you have created, and helps you work with the diverse reactions you and those around you may have to change—particularly the changes you are going to make. **Part Four: A Quick Guide to Mapping** is a streamlined version of the Snapshot process. I put it there for you to return to again and again as you continue to adjust and adapt what you want to create, as well as what life throws your way.

If you are like me and you want to jump right into the process, or you already recognize the value of using visuals to help you set goals, and can't wait to start creating a map to make the changes you need right now, I suggest you go right to **Part Four** and get busy. (You can always flip back to previous parts of the book that go through the process more thoroughly.)

If you are a person who likes context, be sure to read **Part One** before you start the mapping process. Should you be a person who is easily distracted, you will be delighted to know that all sections are short and sweet and the entire book is filled with both stories and facts.

While you could do what *you always do* when you get a book, I encourage you to *do something different*, which is both a great way to start this process and a means to wake your brain up by telling it, "**Pay attention, new things are happening here**!"

Have a great time and shoot me an email at patti@upyourcreativegenius.com to let me know how it went!

PART ONE

WHY MAPPING WORKS: VISUAL IMAGES AND CHANGE

Like a majority of the population, I'm a visual person.[1] When I am working with an individual (or myself) or a business that is navigating big transitions, I use a mapping technique I developed: *"The Snapshot of the Big Picture™"* process. This is a way of examining the current state of your life with a special focus on places where you want to create something new. Once you can capture this in *images*, you begin to create a detailed picture of your desired future reality. Doing this allows you to see, feel and experience what your life will be like when you make some changes. Once you know where you are right now, and where you would like to be in the future, you will build a roadmap to get you from your current to your new destination. Using this visual map, or "Snapshot," you may begin to move toward the life you desire with confidence and clarity.

I have used this process with thousands of people in a wide variety of settings. Although much of my work using the Snapshot process occurred in corporate settings with teams of people, it is just as effective when used by individuals to navigate personal life changes. This book distills my twenty years of working with groups and individuals to give you a concise way to use my method in your own life. It will help you navigate huge earth-shaking changes as well as make small changes to improve the quality of your life. What makes this technique so effective? It incorporates cutting-edge information about how the brain works in such a way that you bypass the parts of your rational mind that tend to sabotage your ability to make positive changes.

On the surface, what I am suggesting may seem simplistic. But this is only because the Snapshot technique communicates directly with the parts of your brain that work with patterns and images. And it is this kind of communication that results in profound, deep-seated changes in how we operate in the world. I have seen it work for thousands of people and I know it will help you, too!

UNDERSTANDING HOW YOUR BRAIN WORKS: A REVIEW

Your brain is divided into two distinct parts that consciously function together to interpret all of your experiences, conscious and unconscious, and to help you understand and react to them. In his book, *A Whole New Mind*, Daniel Pink does a great job of outlining the functions performed by the two sides of the brain.[2]

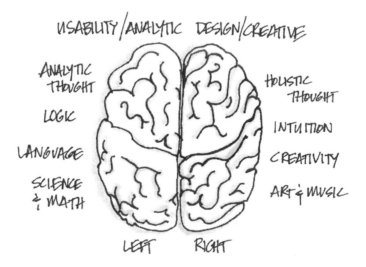

The left side of the brain is associated with a processing style that is sequential and analytic; it recognizes serial events like talking, writing and reading, while the right side of the brain is simultaneous. It tries to find connections and helps us interpret images and emotions. The left is associated with a processing style that is more focused on logical and linear thinking. Right side processing helps focus on context and the big picture. It takes both sides of your brain to help you make decisions and luckily the two work harmoniously to help you access and process information on a number of levels.

To identify where you are in your life at a deep level, you want to consciously activate your brain so you can understand and organize the full picture. By combining words with images, you fire up both sides of your brain simultaneously. Dan Roam's book, *The Back of the Napkin*, illustrates different visual problem-solving methodologies.[3] He describes how the brain integrates information collected from millions of visual signals entering through the retina as photons of light. These signals are transformed into electrical impulses, or signals, that are filtered, compared and categorized to form complete, meaningful pictures. The process your brain uses to absorb information is the same whether you are problem-solving or simply looking an object or scene.

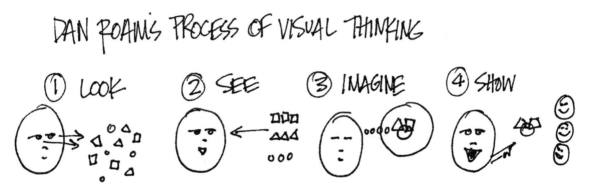

The process of categorizing images and concepts into patterns generates a profound sense of knowing—deeper and stronger than anything the rational mind can create. This synthesizing process is critical for accessing the deep clarity needed to use my Snapshot mapping process.

What brought you to the present moment? What words and images might you use to depict your life experiences? There is always some history or back-story behind them. By creating and examining images as a way of understanding your life, you learn to identify the roads you have been traveling. Some may have taken you to your desired destination; others led to dead ends. In the Snapshot process, we begin with a simple examination of the current state of your life to help you to better understand the "vehicle" you want to drive and the roads you want to travel, as you move into a new landscape that will be the backdrop for your new life.

The part of your mind that keeps driving down the same old roads is your subconscious, which according to cellular biologist Bruce Lipton, author of *The Biology of Belief*, is responsible for about 98 percent of our behavior.[4] Awareness of the way your mind works is the first step to charting a new route. If you pay attention to the thoughts or behaviors that motivate you, you begin to see how they may be sabotaging your life in big and small ways. Are they beliefs from your past that no longer take you in the direction you want to go? If so, are you ready to transform them into new beliefs that will take you towards the future you desire?

OWNING THE LIFE YOU HAVE CREATED

When you step back and look at your life and what you have created, what is and isn't working suddenly comes into clear focus. Because the left side of your brain needs to categorize, it tends to sort experiences into good or bad, comfortable or uncomfortable, and so on. And it brings up a bunch of self-talk; some helpful, some not. The left side of the brain is set up to "critique" how we have been doing, it is wired to compare and contrast and it immediately activates a move toward or get away response[5] that has to do with our internal rewards system. *This is a good thing*, you think to yourself, so your brain directs every part of your system toward creating more of it; or *that experience feels threatening*, thus your brain sends signals to give you less of that.

In fact, any kind of change in our lives causes a reaction. For example, you get a new job; this is considered a "good" change. Most of us, when confronted with a change that we initiated, or one that appears (at least at first) to be better for us, are able to turn on a dime to adapt to the new situation. You like it, it fits into how you have prioritized your internal rewards structure, and subsequently you want to embrace the experience.

But your brain will generate a very different reaction to the job you have been forced to take because you suddenly found yourself unemployed and broke. This feels like a bad change, even if the new job solves a very big problem, because some aspect of it is not aligned with what you want; the commute is horrific or you aren't working in your chosen field, and subsequently you wish you didn't have to take that job and you feel resistant. Internally you want to move away.

This is why some of you who have needed to make a change for a long time have been avoiding it. I am warning you that you can expect to have an initial negative reaction when you begin to use my mapping process to view and examine your current reality. If you are really being honest, you will find it reveals issues that you have been grappling with, often for a very long time.

The Snapshot process will help you find ways to work differently with what you see and you will be surprised at its simplicity and effectiveness. However, no matter what the change is, you will still have to do some work to make things happen.

Suzanne, a participant in a mapping session, wrote about what happened when she worked on the Current Reality part of her map. "It put into a visual context what I know about myself. Seeing the fear component in my images challenges me to look at this piece with compassion and courage so I can make the desired changes. This has been my focus now, building my confidence." She is a great example of someone willing to look at, and work with, self-made obstacles. It isn't easy to dig deep enough to understand what might be contributing to any internal dissonance.

But you can bet, if you don't do something about the dissonance you feel, you will end up being forced to. Do you hate your current administrative job because what you really want to do is be a chef? Do your find your primary relationship boring? Do you feel you never have time to relax? If so, you might find yourself spending long hours on the couch recovering from a sprained ankle.

In other words, you can count on life to do something to provide you with the changes you need, even if you are not consciously asking for them to happen. In the mapping process, you will find it can be empowering to admit your part in creating how you got to where you are today. Look without judgment at both what is working and what isn't, to see that just below the surface of your perceptions lies the truth. The more you own your truth, the easier it will be to transform into something that aligns more closely with your goals.

A workshop participant had recently gotten a DUI. He explained his situation to me and then expressed with exasperation, "Well, how was I supposed to know that they lowered the blood alcohol level in our state?" Often we make our situations more difficult by not looking at the full picture to see what we have created through our beliefs and actions. When we fail to do the hard work of examining the truth, we prolong the process of changing, and make it much more difficult. The truth was, he drank too much to legally and safely drive, yet he chose to drive anyway. It was as simple as that!

When life takes an unexpected turn, it is easy to ask, "Why did this happen to me?" If you really want to change your current situation, you must also change the behavior that set in motion the pattern that created your situation. It may be wiser to ask, "What is life trying to tell me about myself through this experience?" When you ask this question in response to life's changes, you begin getting answers that allow you to assess honestly where you are and clues for how to go about charting a new course.

Because in truth, change is a constant process. It is only our perception of the change that makes it seem good or bad. Your goal when you begin to depict the Current Reality portion of your map will be to raise your level of awareness so you become responsible, without judgment, guilt or regret, for what you have created. Simply observe, and note, the patterns with openness and curiosity.

We tend to repeat patterns because they are part of a learned behavior that was solidified in our brains early in life. In a workshop I took to understand a process called Psych-K[6], a participant shared her disdain for doing dishes. When the facilitator probed her a bit, the woman recalled that her mother had once slapped her face when she had done a poor job of dish washing. The facilitator explained, "The subconscious doesn't know about time. Each time you stand in front of the sink or think about doing your dishes it is as if your mother just slapped you a second ago." Her task was to reprogram that part of her subconscious to bring it up to date. Your experiences planted the seeds of your present reactions. By creating a map of where you are now, you can uncover life events that established your beliefs and behaviors, decide if they no longer serve you, and choose to change them.

DREAM A DESIRED NEW REALITY

Okay, 'fess up. Are you a perpetual daydreamer? Why shouldn't you be? It's exciting to dream of what we would like to be doing or having in our world. A recent *New York Times* article[7] examined how letting your mind wander actually helps you to remain focused on your key goals instead of getting mired in the dull details that accompany consciousness.

When you are preoccupied with a routine task, the part of your mind that is "daydreaming" is actually focusing on your bigger picture goals. Daydreaming or mind-wandering helps bring into focus those things that are your bigger priorities and long-term goals, and helps keep them from getting lost in a sea of short-term objectives, like today's "to-do" list.

When you daydream, you enter a heightened state of problem-solving that also makes you happy. You might be surprised by this: studies of the habits of highly successful men indicate that the one thing they all had in common was the tendency to daydream when faced with challenging problems.[8]

When you daydream, you send signals to your subconscious that whatever you are dreaming about is something you would like to see happen.

Repeated daydreaming about something seems to reprogram your brain and tells your mind where to put its focus and attention. This method for programming success has been used for years by professional athletes. Anyone can do it.

A series of events in my life convinced me of the power of my imagination and inner visualization. Many years ago, I was living in New York City and taking acting classes. Like many starving artists, I would sometimes do street theater to make a little spare change. I had come up with a short comic routine using a Michael Jackson song that was very popular at the time. The piece started with a comic monologue followed by my transforming myself into a tennis player who pulled a tennis racket out of a toy baby buggy, all the while lip syncing, "Billie Jean is not my lover, she's just a girl who thinks that I am the one, but the kid is not my son, no no no, no no no, OOOOH!"

What can I say? I'm a performance artist! One day, after passing the hat, I ended up with a grand total of $9.68, not bad for fifteen minutes of work. And it was just enough to buy a couple slices of pizza, two cokes and subway tokens back to my fourth-floor walk-up in Brooklyn's Park Slope!

As I walked downtown with a friend in search of the best cheap pizza, we passed through the Broadway theatre district. My friend asked me if I ever wanted to perform on Broadway. "Me?" I replied with a laugh, "I'm a performance artist. I would only perform *off-Broadway*."

But later, his question haunted me and I began to wonder what it would feel like to perform on Broadway. I let myself fantasize about walking through the stage door entrance and into a dressing room with my name on the door. I saw my costume spread out on my dressing table, and watched myself dress and apply my makeup. I heard the call for "places" as I waited silently behind the thick velvet curtain for the house lights to go down. I heard that quiet, expectant hush just before the curtain rises and felt my own anticipation as I went onstage.

I told myself to snap out of it. But the lingering sensations of my Broadway fantasy gave me chills. The next time I found myself daydreaming about it, I let myself go even further. If I'm going to be performing on Broadway, I tried to imagine where our opening night party might be. Hmmm, I think, maybe Tavern on the Green! At this point my imagination is going wild and I imagine who might be in the audience. What stars might I get to meet when they came backstage to offer their congratulations for my amazing performance? I pictured meeting comic greats like Robin Williams or Steve Martin. My Broadway dream was great fun and it sustained me as I continued to deal with the decidedly unglamorous reality of my life as a struggling performer in the Big Apple.

Eventually I left New York and returned home to Seattle where my career as a performance artist sank to an all-time low. I was so broke I really did not know what I was going to do. All of the regular funding sources for my work, foundation grants and government programs, had dried up. My mother's poor health required me to travel frequently to Los Angeles and even my meager shifts at a local Mexican restaurant had been cut to the bone. I had no idea how I was going to pay my rent. I found myself daydreaming about an alternate reality where I was a Broadway performer and it was a wonderful escape.

One day, in total desperation, but convinced that I could somehow pull a rabbit out of the hat, I came up with a plan to generate some much-needed cash. I grabbed a rake and drove towards one of the wealthiest neighborhoods in Seattle. Putting my best foot forward, I started knocking on doors and offering to rake yards for the bargain price of $10 per yard.

Unfortunately, as a performance artist I had dyed my hair a weird orange color, which meant that no one wanted to open their door, let alone pay me to rake their yards. Running out of houses, I knocked on the door of the Presbyterian Church where a clever minister gladly hired me to rake his "yard" that was about the size of a small football field. It was a typical day in Seattle: rainy and windy. As the wind blew leaves as fast as I raked them, my efforts were futile and after almost three hours, I had only half the yard raked. Finally the minister took pity on me, gave a ten-dollar bill and sent me on my way. Tired, wet and discouraged, and with only ten lousy dollars to show for my heroic efforts, I drove home feeling worse than ever.

At home, I had two messages waiting for me: one from a friend telling me about auditions being held for performance artists at the Seattle Repertory Theatre and encouraging me to audition; and another from my long-lost agent, whom I hadn't heard from in almost three years, telling me about the same audition. She added that the auditions were for an upcoming show with the comedian Bill Irwin.

Even though I had sworn in the past that I would never perform anyone else's material, I decided to give it a try. I felt hopeful and nervous as I stood in line the next day waiting my turn. The audition involved doing a weird little hop-skip dance step. I panicked: I'm not a dancer! I did my best, as Bill Irwin and Nance, his production stage manager watched. My years of experience with comic improvisation resulted in a quirky interpretation of the dance steps. Suddenly, I found myself with a part in the show. And then the magic began. Our show moved from the small theater to the main stage of the Seattle Repertory Theatre. Six months later, we performed at the Kennedy Center in Washington, DC. And finally, we ended up, guess where? On Broadway!

It keeps getting better! Our opening night was held at the Tavern on the Green, and when we went for drinks to celebrate our success, whom did we see? Steve Martin! And then during the course of our run on Broadway my fantasies were complete the night Robin Williams came backstage to meet the cast.

Was this all an amazing coincidence? I believe that the pictures I conjured up over and over in my mind, that series of visuals, started the process of making it all real. And so I can say with complete conviction, what begins as a simple daydream can become reality.

Reflect back on your own personal accomplishments. How many of your goals began as a simple idea that you played around with in your mind before you took action to achieve it?

SHIFT INTO A POSITIVE FRAME OF MIND

While your imagination is the springboard for ideas, you also need a positive, non-critical environment that allows you to gain the most benefit from what you imagine. Our positive and negative beliefs affect every part of our body and our life.[9] To dream about your Desired New Reality, you must first put yourself into an open state of mind that will give you an unlimited playing field in which to draw up the new you. You want to imagine and envision the best-case scenario for achieving whatever you desire. To think and act creatively and get the full benefit of your imagination, you have to be willing to create and absorb information non-judgmentally. You can develop and expand your ability to brainstorm through what is called your "absorb brainset"[10]—that part of your brain that helps you take in externally or internally generated ideas or information with an uncritical eye. One way to "up your creative genius" when you find yourself starting to get critical is to simply become more curious.

Another way to clear your head and prepare yourself to step into new thinking in a positive way is to *do something out of the ordinary*, or even slightly uncomfortable. When you encounter something unfamiliar or new, you interrupt the movement of thoughts as they travel along their accustomed neural pathways. This is something you may have experienced when you traveled to an unfamiliar place. Suddenly you are aware of yourself in a way that is dramatically different from your usual sense of self. This shift is key when you are trying to expand your brainwaves and generate breakthrough ideas. You also want to take the time to consciously set a positive intent about what you are about to experience, as it will result in your having a better outcome.[11]

What you do to create an environment that helps you shift to a positive state of mind will be unique to you, so experiment with a few of these ideas. A simple change you can make is to turn off electronic devices such as the TV, radio, computer and, of course, your phone. Then become more aware of your surroundings. Listen to the sounds around you. Notice the colors of the room or the texture of the chair you are sitting in. Do a few jumping jacks or run around to work up a sweat. Shift where you are sitting to another part of your office or house. Finally, before you begin, shut your eyes for a minute to remove external stimulation and remind yourself that you are about to walk into this next experience with openness and curiosity. Closing your eyes helps your brain prepare; it organizes what you already know from the past and reorders it to help you focus on what you are about to do,[12] like reshuffling the card deck of your experiences.

WHEN DAYDREAMS AND PLANS GET TOGETHER

Many years ago, I was just starting my career as a drama therapist and working on my business plan. I had racked up quite a bit of debt in graduate school and was eager to kick-start my business, so I asked my friend Michael to help me set some goals around manifesting money. He had a successful sales career and was skilled at achieving financial goals; he was the perfect person to teach me how to create my own goal-setting plan.

I remember our meeting as if it happened yesterday. It was a typically beautiful, sunny day in Northern California. As we sat on my patio, he asked, "So Patti, how much money do you want to make next year? Write it down on that piece of paper." He pushed a piece of paper towards me. This completely freaked me out. I was immediately worried about what he would think of me if I told him a number that was too high or too low. I was still so limited in what

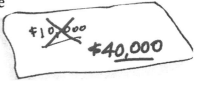

I thought I could manifest that I wrote down $10,000.00, thinking to myself, "That seems possible." He looked at the number and then at me and said, "What would happen if you

decided you wanted to make four times that amount?" He reached over and changed my 10K to 40K. My jaw dropped. How would that ever be possible? As a new graduate, the most I could hope for was some kind of entry-level work in my field. I remember laughing a nervous little laugh, and saying, "Uh, okay, if you say so!" Then with the utmost confidence he said, "Now I'm going to show you how to do it."

By using my calendar, and asking me a series of questions, he began to write down how many clients or jobs I would need to meet my goal. He helped me identify how many jobs I would have to do per month, how much money I thought I could charge per job, and then how many jobs I would need to do per week … and just like that, after only an hour, I had a plan. He gently and firmly walked me through those simple, basic steps. And though I had no idea how I would actually do what he proposed, I was struck by the fact that he believed I could do it, and before long, so did I!

In the following months, I followed through with my plan, faithfully calculating the number of jobs I needed to reach my goal. I was excited and confident. I knew exactly what I needed to do in order to reach my financial goals and so I diligently worked each step to make them real. One year later my total income was $38,500.00! Almost exactly four times what I first imagined possible on that bright sunny day. By the end of the year, I was a true believer in setting simple, actionable steps. (Thanks, Michael!)

In addition to assessing where you are now and allowing yourself to dream about what you would like to see happen, you must ground your Snapshot with a clear action plan that will help keep you pointed in the right direction, and give you a way to measure (and celebrate) your progress.

A plan also keeps us aware of the fact that most of the time it takes slow, determined actions to move us away from people and situations that don't feel right. This is important to remember, as we all have a tendency to want change to happen instantaneously. Once we realize we are done with our current situation and are ready to move on, there is often a bit of lag time before the Desired New Reality becomes apparent. During this pause, one of two things may happen: we can make abrupt, sometimes ill-advised changes to satisfy the need to do something different; or, we can become so overwhelmed by the enormity of the task before us that, well, it may seem easier to put up with things as they are.

The tendency to avoid change at the start of a new venture happens a lot. A study showed that even when faced with a life-or-death situation that required change in order to survive, the odds that the person would actually embrace the needed change were nine to one. Only one out of ten people will *actually make that change.*[13] One out of ten!

Who is that one person who actually integrates the information that clearly indicates big changes are needed, and then takes action? According to the same study, it is someone who both believes and expects that they can make the necessary changes. When we hear stories of prison inmates who left jail to lead productive lives, heart attack survivors who completely changed their lifestyle and diet, or people who confronted and recovered from huge emotional losses with effective therapy and support groups, the underlying keys to their success were *belief* and *expectation*.

While these are key critical components, I would add that belief and expectation are the direct result of our ability to conjure an image of the change we desire, record it in our mind's eye, and to create a plan to bring it into being. It's one thing to *say* we want to change, or know that we *should* change, but it's something else to actually be able to picture ourselves doing everything needed to get there. Creating a picture in your mind enhances your beliefs and expectations because the imagery process reroutes the brain so it works in a new way.[14] And this, in turn, reveals the steps you need to take to dig in and get your hands dirty.

A number of consultants I know work for firms that require them to work many more hours each week than I do. They also have shorter vacations and spend many more days traveling around the world to work with their clients. One of my regular collaborators often says to me, "I want your life!" What he means is, "I want to be able to go biking or hiking whenever I feel like it." I remind him that he can have my life. He just needs to reorganize his workload, get an assistant to handle mundane tasks, and convince his boss that a balance between work and personal time results in more creative solutions.

The truth is that even if he were to make these suggestions, if he doesn't really believe his boss will go for it, or that he could make enough money if he cut back on work hours, it is likely that he will stay where he is. In short, if he can't imagine it happening, he will continue to be frustrated by the demands of his work, longing for more free time, and unable to envision or expect anything else to happen. Your ability to create a new reality for yourself is completely dependent on two things: your *desire* for change; and your *belief* in your ability to make change happen. When these two things are stronger than your belief that you can't change, movement begins.

Belief and desire give birth to the expectations that feed your dream. And all of these spring to life in your imagination. Envisioning what you want, and using the Snapshot mapping process to create a visual depiction of your goals will set all of this in motion. For this reason, it is important to do each step of the mapping process described in the next part of this book. By using your brain in a new way, you begin to see things differently, which allows new solutions to emerge.

ADDING TO YOUR PICTURE OF SUCCESS

If your daydreaming results in some surprises, you may need to do a bit of work to match your visions with a clear picture of what is involved. Information gathering will help you do this. For example, if you think that your perfect job would be as a web designer, or some other work that requires hours and hours of computer time, and you have never actually spent weeks sitting and staring at a computer, you might need to adjust your goals. And if you are also an extrovert who loves being in front of a room of people, well, you might need to make some adjustments to bring everything into alignment before you set a plan in motion to launch your new career as a web designer.

Interview a few people who live the life you imagine to find out the pros and cons. In other words, the more information you have about what your life would look like when you succeed in your goal, the better. What you don't want to do is dedicate your vision and intention toward creating a life that isn't what you really wanted.

When I first saw a strategic illustrator draw a real-time picture on a big piece of butcher paper in a business-planning meeting, something clicked inside. I knew this was something I could do and that I wanted to explore. But before I made any kind of commitment to walk down this path, I needed to try it out to see if I liked it. And, even though I *thought* I might be able to do it, I wanted to be certain.

So how did I go about it? First, I looked for an opportunity to do strategic illustrating in a real meeting. I emailed every consultant I knew until I found someone willing to give me a chance to try my hand at capturing, in words and images, one of their sessions. My friend Trudy was going to facilitate a meeting with a group of churches working to find common ground for future projects. She asked me to "scribe" or capture what was being discussed in the meeting. She thought I would be simply using colored pens and a flip chart to keep track of the words and ideas from the group discussion. I had something a bit more intricate in mind: I was planning to draw little pictures in the margins as I'd seen the strategic illustrator do at the meeting that inspired me.

When I started scribing the meeting notes, something surprising happened. I began to draw pictures of the participants and their ideas, and interspersed with the pictures were the words they were using. It was so much fun I lost myself! My images were fairly basic, but the final "notes" looked cool and the group loved it! In fact, their first shared group experience was their unanimous appreciation of the strange, colorful graphics I had created. They all agreed that they loved my notes, even though they found they had opposing views on just about everything else!

This experience made it real for me. It showed me that I could draw the kinds of pictures that the strategic illustrator had used (as basic and archaic as my images might have been), and people appreciated and found value in seeing their words portrayed graphically. I realized that I had discovered something that might provide me with an interesting, creative and financially viable career. Trudy thought my illustrations were a great addition to her facilitation and she continued to hire me whenever she could.

In the meantime, I expanded my drawing skills by interning for an advanced graphic recorder/strategic illustrator. I also kept my day job as a drama therapist until I felt I had enough work to do graphic recording and consulting full time. A year later, I moved to Colorado to join forces with another graphic recorder and started a new career that just a short time before had only existed on the Desired New Reality side of my personal map. To get there I had to let myself imagine what was possible, even though I had no idea how to make it all happen, and then take specific steps to find out what it would look and feel like to actually manifest my desires. My research confirmed that this was the job for me, and then everything else unfolded, leading me to my goal.

SET SUCCESS MEASURES: REVISIT, REVISE & CELEBRATE

To build your strategy for creating what you want, you need to be focused and you must also take action. You can wish your life would change all you want, but until you actually step forward to do something to make it happen, everything you long for will simply be a pipe dream. Lots of people spend their lives dreaming about doing something else. Crossing the chasm that separates where you are now from where you wish you were requires taking that scary first step. Sometimes the first step is to simply draw out all of the images in your head to see what is real and what is not.

This process can happen anywhere, at any time. I frequently travel on planes where I find my fellow travelers are more than willing to share all sorts of details about themselves with me. Why not? They know chances are very slim we will ever see each other again. And, because I am naturally curious about people, I like to engage them in conversation, which helps me keep my finger on the pulse of what others are dealing with as they move through life. I am amazed at how often the person sitting next to me is in the midst of some kind of major life transition. Out of the blue, they will often start to describe what I have learned to recognize as *the telltale signs that their lives need to change.*

The conversation may start with them telling me that they don't like their job, are confused about what to do with their life, or wonder about their purpose. Sometimes they talk about relationships. Whatever the topic, certain feelings come up again and again in the words they use to describe their lives: *stuck, lost, worried or wishing they had, did, or were something or someone else.*

While they talk, I draw a Mini-Map for them; a map just like the one you will create in the next chapter, except it hones in on that one problem you are most focused on—thus the term "Mini-Map." A Mini-Map helps you re-focus and often gives you instant perspective and sometimes, instant relief. After just a short plane ride conversation, I would hand my fellow passenger the drawing I created. By the time we parted, they were usually smiling and confident that there was a way to change that part of their life that wasn't working.

For me, and the people I work with, mapping is the easy part. The hard part is to keep focused on those goals, and carry out all the steps needed to transform a desire into a plan. Some maps include Desired New Realities that take days or weeks to be realized, while others may take years. Staying with the process and working step by step will be easier if you keep track of all the tiny shifts that move you closer to your goals, and celebrate each advance you make.

Your timeline for achieving the goals you depict will be hard to predict. The only thing I have noticed is that the speed at which change occurs seems to depend on the amount of risk you can afford to take. If your goal is to quit your job and you have a family to support, you'll have to have a solid plan in place before you dump your current job. If you long to attract a new romantic partner, this may end up at the bottom of your list while you sort out the relationship you are in, or work to discover the reason you aren't attracting the kind of partner you desire. The more you can define what success looks like for you, the easier it is to know you are on track toward accomplishing one of your goals.

LEVERAGE THE MOST POWERFUL ACCELERATOR YOU HAVE: YOUR IMAGINATION

Over the years I have found that when I envision something I want to manifest, or accomplish, and then continue to enhance my vision by using my imagination, it inevitably comes to be. Imagining what will be makes the whole process more fun.

You are born with the innate gift of imagination. When we are young, we use it freely. When children play, they spontaneously create entire worlds of imaginary friends, places and adventures. Children are also likely to join together to create imaginary situations in which they all join in the creation process. As we get older, we tend to get more selective in the ways we use our imagination. The biggest change is that imagination becomes a very private activity that surfaces from time to time for no particular purpose. If you find yourself stuck in a horrible traffic jam, you may imagine yourself suddenly stepping on the gas and ramming your way out, pushing all the other cars aside. Or you may meet someone new who seems interesting and you imagine falling in love with them, or having them hire you for a prestigious job making tons of money. In other words, adult imaginings tend to be fleeting amusements, unless you harness them and put them to work for you. The more you engage your imagination in conjunction with your vision of what you desire, the more you will find how truly powerful your IQ or Imagination Quotient really is. Dr. Wendy Masi conducted a number of studies that showed the Imagination Quotient is one of key predictors in a child's academic success.[15]

Here is an equation I call *The Plus Factor*:

$$\text{Imagination} \times \text{Intuition} + \text{Desire} \times \text{Drive} = \text{Outcome}^4$$

A colleague and I developed *The Plus Factor* to explain the process activated when you consciously multiply the power of your imagination by incorporating your intuition, then add your desire for that future state (the emotion or feeling behind it) and multiply all of this by your drive, or the energy you put into taking action on your plan. All of this equals a substantial exponential increase in your expected outcome.

Accessing your imagination, and allowing yourself to play with your vision helps fuel your desire to achieve your goal. The drive part is literally you, especially when you are generating chemicals in your brain, like serotonin, that are produced whenever you feel elated about your vision. And the momentum toward your Desired New Reality will only increase as you follow through on the Bold Steps you will identify in the next chapter.

BUILD TRUST

Do you trust that your dreams really will occur? Are you a glass half-empty person, or glass half-full kind of dreamer? What beliefs do you hold? Do you feel we live in a loving world filled with challenges to help us learn and grow? Or do you hold a belief that the world is unfair and unjust? It's hard to feel you are making progress when you feel powerless to change your circumstances.

Recently I spoke with a man who wasn't certain he was going to get the job he had applied for. When he asked me what he should do, I replied, "Don't worry, if you don't get this one, it's because you'll get something better." He didn't hesitate before stating, "I don't believe that." I immediately recognized that nothing I could say or do was going to change his patterned belief. Beliefs only change as a result of our own direct experience.

If you feel stuck and victimized by what you are experiencing, ask yourself, "What's the payoff I am getting from this belief? Is it really working for me? How do I benefit from complaining about my situation? Am I open to testing my theory and trying something new?"

Unfortunately, many of our beliefs about the world are based on and built around fear. To counter fear, call on belief and trust. They are fresh air for the resilient change agent to breathe. The more you take in belief and trust, the stronger your dream becomes. If you do not trust that things will manifest for you, they simply won't. Even if you are a trusting person, your belief that the universe is operating on your behalf will be challenged when you are diagnosed with a grave illness or suffer the unexpected loss of a loved one.

Elisabeth Kübler-Ross, one of my early heroes who did ground-breaking work helping people with life-threatening illnesses accept and embrace death, changed what she was doing after her own mother died. Her mother had been a very giving woman throughout her entire life, taking care of her husband and the rest of the family during hard times. At the end of her mother's life, a severe stroke incapacitated her, she had to rely on others to be fed and bathed. It was a big challenge for this highly competent woman who had always been the one to care for herself and others. Her mother lived for three long months like this before she was able to transition out of this life. Kübler-Ross was frustrated and tortured to see her mother in such a debilitated state. It was evident that her mother felt humiliated by her own helplessness and need for such extensive care. In her prayers, Kübler-Ross railed against God asking, "Why? Why are you making my mother suffer so after she has taken care of all of us and selflessly served her whole family for her entire life?"

Months after her mother's passing, her bitterness towards God making it difficult to work, Kübler-Ross shared her anger and frustration with a Buddhist monk. She was surprised when he said, "Just think how wonderful it was that it only took three months for your mother to balance out a life-time's worth of caring for other people." His comment was a wake-up call for Kübler-Ross, and she suddenly saw what an amazing and mysterious experience life is.[16] Some pieces of our life's mystery are revealed to us right in the moment they occur; others take time and a new perspective to become clear. Life becomes much easier when you allow yourself to have a little faith and trust. Believe things will work out just as they should and trust that you will know what to do each step of the way. Be curious rather than resistant. Your openness will make room for greater insight.

Of course there are real reasons why we struggle to find these insights and to hold on to faith and trust. The left side of your brain doesn't always realize when things are being handled in the right way or within the perfect time frame. When things don't happen in a snap, we may revert back to old ways of thinking or behaving. Like we stand in our garden shaking our fist at the big "up there" in the sky, asking when will things happen our way?

You are the only one who can create the opening, or internal space, for new light to pass through. One way to create a bigger opening is to get quiet inside. Someone reflected to me, "Getting quiet is the only true spiritual path; it breaks through all that rigidity to hear what you might need to do next." Another way to create an opening is to take a walk by yourself (without your headphones and music) watching and listening to the things you pass.

Discover your own ways to create stillness if you want to see the actual pattern or bigger system you are participating in. Be present and grateful for what is occurring right now. This releases your hold on how things need to happen and increases your ability to catch the subtle nuance of where you are and what you might do next.

FLEXIBILITY AND ADAPTABILITY

Children are in a constant state of adaptation and growth, but as you age, you sometimes become fixed in your ways of thinking and tend to get in familiar routines. You can get stiff and inflexible on many levels. To embrace and adapt to change, you have to get back in shape. How can you keep in the best shape for change? By flexing your change muscles through initiating small changes in your life on a regular basis. This can be as simple as doing one thing differently every day to create new patterns in your behavior. Changes big or small make you respond differently and force your brain to learn something new. These little changes can be as simple as driving a different route to work or home, having tea instead of coffee a couple of mornings a week, or moving your favorite chair so that you have a different view out of the window.

One of my European colleagues works for a global manufacturing company that requires him and his family to move to a different country every few years. He is the con-summate change agent: enthusiastic, outgoing and creative. I have long admired his ability to remain flexible and engaged while constantly facing new and unfamiliar situations. Although I know he excels at doing this in his work setting, I was curious about how these changes affected his personal life. I asked him how his wife and sons deal with the frequent moves. He explained that because they have little control over the actual place they are moving to, he involves them in making as many other decisions as possible. For example, before the family moves, his wife visits the new city and chooses their house, neighbor-hood, and schools. His children, who now speak five different languages and claim to only care about the sports teams in their new schools, are encouraged to take an active role in deciding what their new lives in a new city will look like. It appears to me that he has cre-ated flexibility in his family's ability to adapt to frequent change. They experience changes as exciting new opportunities and are open to new things because they have the power to make decisions about what they feel is best for them. When everyone has a role to play and all ideas are considered, the process of navigating changes becomes something everyone participates in, not just a problem they are forced to accept.

On a larer scale, I know that companies and organizations also struggle to adapt to change. In many cases, they have invested a lot of money in a particular product or strategy and the risk of trying something new might affect their profits. One company I work with appeared extremely fixed in the way they did things. In annual mapping sessions with their top management team, I noticed that they were very resistant to making changes to the style of map we used to chart their new goals. They would just change the content of the map, but not the image. When they got ready to use the same exact style for the fifth year in a row, I drew a number of other suggested metaphors to help them find a different perspective for their challenges. They hated my new ideas and told me they wanted to revert to their old tried and true map style. During a break in our mapping sessions, I toured their manufacturing plant, where I noticed that some of the ways they did things seemed old and outdated, while in other areas they were shifting and moving with the market. It dawned on me that what was happening in our mapping session was also occurring throughout the company. Because they were not willing to consider sweeping changes to their normal way of doing things, they were stuck. The parts of the company that were highly structured and somewhat outdated were holding back the parts of the company that were trying to innovate new methods. The tension between the two conflicting ways of doing business appeared to be the core of what needed addressing.

Back in the session after the tour, I shared my perceptions with them. After a long silence, one of the team leaders proposed a new Bold Step that would require everyone to consider that they create a totally new way of solving their challenges. Immediately, the team responded with enthusiasm and ideas and we soon created a radically new map to guide them for the year ahead.

LET GO OF THE PAST TO STEP FULLY INTO THE FUTURE

When I was sobbing in the garden about the hacked-up lemon tree, I finally realized that I was letting go of thinking of myself as an actor—even though at that moment I couldn't imagine what that meant. Acting was all I ever wanted to do. If I wasn't an actor, what was left? Somehow, maybe due to pure exhaustion from all that crying, I begin to relax my grip on the past and this slight shift created a little tiny opening for the next thing to emerge.

That very night, I had coffee with some casual friends. When one of them heard the sad story about my non-existent acting career, he asked if I had ever heard of the Drama Therapy program at the California Institute of Integral Studies in San Francisco. Had I ever considered going back to school? Since I had really let go of my acting aspirations once and for all, I was open to his suggestion. So much so, that I contacted the school the next morning only to discover that "coincidentally" there was an informational meeting being held at the school the next night.

Now if someone had pulled me aside and said, "Okay Patti, first you're going to be an actor, go to Broadway, then have an artistic breakdown which leads you to taking an axe to people's gardens, until finally one day you will go back to school to become a drama therapist," I would have said, "What??"

I had never considered graduate school. I'd earned my bachelor's degree at a very progressive college full of hippies, where we never wrote term papers, sat in circles on the ground for class lectures, and didn't get grades. Higher education was not in my future vision at all.

The next night at the informational meeting, one of the students enrolled in the Drama Therapy program described how she ended up there. She told us she'd been an actor for many years and had loved the career. She thrived with the challenges of new roles, and exploring new ideas. She had been very successful. Then she got some bad reviews and suddenly what other people said about her meant more than what she thought about herself, until the day she just couldn't do it anymore.

It was almost as if she was speaking for me, as this was exactly what I was feeling inside. In that moment I knew that the next step for me involved going back to school to become a Drama Therapist. Within 48 hours I had gone from utter despair and hopelessness, letting go of my identity, only to have something new show up that was better than anything I could have imagined. All I had to do was step through that new doorway to heal myself.

Exercise: Examining What's Not Being Said

Where do you begin to change self-defeating behaviors? How can you release old ways of doing things? First, examine the ways you are currently doing things and see if there is anything unspoken that's keeping you from changing. As a change agent, I work with a simple technique, which looks like this:

In the top part of the triangle, you put the Said, those things you are saying on the surface about what's happening around you. In the bottom of the triangle you put the Unsaid, those subterranean thoughts and feelings that lie behind what's being said.

The "Said" might be, "We have a great relationship," while the "Unsaid" might be, "Except he drinks too much." The Said might be, "I love my job," and the Unsaid is, "I gotta put up with that damn commute everyday." The Said is, "We value our friends," and the Unsaid is, "But we don't really have time to connect with them."

There is always more to the picture than meets the eye. In the next chapter you will be creating a visual representation, and these Unsaids will help you understand and work with what has really been going on. Surfacing and reviewing what you have been avoiding helps everything become more open and pliable. By owning your history, you become empowered to do what is needed in the future.

EXPLORE YOUR OPTIONS

Once you have had a chance to work through what's in your way, it's time to help prepare yourself for looking at what you want to do next. The question of what is going to happen next is unknown, and possibly risky, but it is also a huge opportunity. If you are in fight-or-flight mode, you won't be able to take charge of what is happening. The fight-or-flight response, a term first coined by Walter Bradford Cannon, is an acute stress response that helps protect you against something fearful—like a charging animal that wants you for dinner, causing you to either stand and fight or run for your life. Fearful or new situations can elicit this response and interrupt your ability to think clearly when taking action or making decisions. You simply react, and that is not a particularly effective way to create positive change. Women under stress do not always experience the fight or flight response in this way due to hormonal differences. A UCLA study conducted in 2003[17] showed women under stress elicit a "tend or befriend" response. Women characteristically reach out and gather rather those nearest and dearest, nurture self and help those in need, even if strangers. This response can also be a distraction if you spend too much time processing what you've been doing and not focusing on your options moving forward.

Exploring your options means just that, looking at all of the things you could be doing now and in the future instead of what you have been doing in the past.

Exercise: Exploring Your Options

This next exercise is going to help set you up for success in the mapping process. Start by taking a blank sheet of paper and listing all the things you already know that exist as future possibilities. Make sure you capture a little detail around them, such as the pros and cons of each of these options from your perspective. Then flip your paper over. On the backside, you are going to pretend you are someone else: someone you admire, or an imaginary you who is not limited by time and space or financial constraints. All things you have already listed on the other side of your paper are your "in the box" ideas.

Now it's time to get out of your own mind's box. Close your eyes briefly to block out any stimulation from your surroundings. Imagine someone taking your hand and beginning to write what is best for you right now. What will stretch you in a new direction and break you out of your pattern? Write across the top of the paper, "Show me my next step." Then, let your hand start writing—beginning with anything that comes to you. It might start off with "This is stupid." Keep writing. Keep asking the questions, "What do you want me to do? What is my next step? What can I do now that is more in line with my true purpose? If there is a better step for me, what is it?" Keep writing until you have at least three pages of ideas. Then go back and circle the ones that seem interesting to explore. Identify which of these you may want to focus on in your map. Keep these ready for when you imagine your Desired New Reality in the next chapter.

Exploring your options is a freeing activity that shifts you out of the known into the unknown. In the unknown, there are new truths to be found about yourself, your capabilities, and what could become new beliefs. The experience of creating a new world for yourself, despite how you came to this moment in time, will be much more pleasant if you can keep pushing yourself into the unfamiliar to find what is right for you now. Water rises to its own level. How high can you rise as you explore what is possible for you?

PRACTICE THE NEW YOU

You have explored and uncovered what was unsaid about the changes you are experiencing. Now you will find you have new information and perhaps a better understanding of a pattern or what has been driving a particular choice. To create something new in your world takes ingenuity, which includes unfamiliar action steps, and as they say, "practice makes perfect."

A colleague mentioned this in passing about his newly formed relationship: his partner told him he had never before asked for what he wanted in his relationships. It hadn't ever felt like an option. I thought about it a moment and then asked if he wanted any suggestions. He did, so I offered, "You might practice having him ask for something he wants from you every few days. It will help him anchor the feeling into his body and create the new pathway in his brain."

Practice how you'd like yourself to behave before you get into something new. The brain is wired in such a way that you don't even have to practice the behavior outwardly for it to imprint. You can practice it over and over again in your mind. Your brain cannot distinguish between what is real and what is imaginary.[18] To me, this is the beauty of understanding the new brain science and how your brain works. It gives you the freedom to prepare, using your imagination, for what you will experience in reality.

Actors review their lines and the internal beats of a scene over and over again until they can routinely hit their emotional mark at the right moment. With that knowledge firmly embedded in their body, they feel secure that they can always be in the right state of mind when performing. If they were to lose their lines on stage, they could still retain the core emotion of the scene.

While you might mentally forget the process of staying curious and inquisitive when things get strained, practicing your desired behavior ahead of time will help you make a different choice. Take a deep breath and then imagine yourself successfully controlling your emotions during a potentially difficult interaction. When that moment occurs in reality, you will be surprised to find that you can actually respond the way you practiced in your mind. Changing behavior takes both inner and outer practice, but with enough effort, it can happen automatically.

A FINAL PLUG FOR VISUALS

New brain discoveries are happening all the time, and one fact is often repeated. Your brain will remember the emotional components of an experience better than any other aspect or details. As time goes on, you'll recall only the gist of things.

> *"At least part, and perhaps much of what we see is changed, interpreted, or conceptualized in ways that depend on a person's training, mind-set, and past experiences. We tend to see what we expect to see or what we decide we have seen. This expectation or decision, however, often is not a conscious process. Instead, the brain frequently does the expecting and deciding, without our conscious awareness, and then alters or rearranges—or even simply disregards—the raw data of vision that hits the retina.*
>
> *Learning perception through drawing seems to change this process and to allow a different, more direct kind of seeing. The brain's editing is somehow put on hold, thereby permitting one to see more fully and perhaps more realistically... This new way of seeing may alone be reason enough to learn to draw."*
>
> ~ Betty Edwards, *The New Drawing on the Right Side of the Brain*

Part One has given your brain context and shown it where to tune in and prepare for what you are about to do. Because the brain will lose details over time, what will keep the process locked into your long-term memory are the pictures or symbols you create to augment or replace the words you will use. Those images will give the ideas and contents of your map emotional charge. That charge is what will help propel you away from the things you want to let go of and towards those things you desire.

Remember, if you find yourself resisting the idea of using pictures, think of whence you came—the first recorded language was visual, as in cave drawings. Visuals are part of your DNA; once you relax and use them, you will see how pictures can guide and inspire you. It's time to get them working for you.

PART TWO

THE MAPPING PROCESS: CURRENT REALITY BECOMES DESIRED NEW REALITY

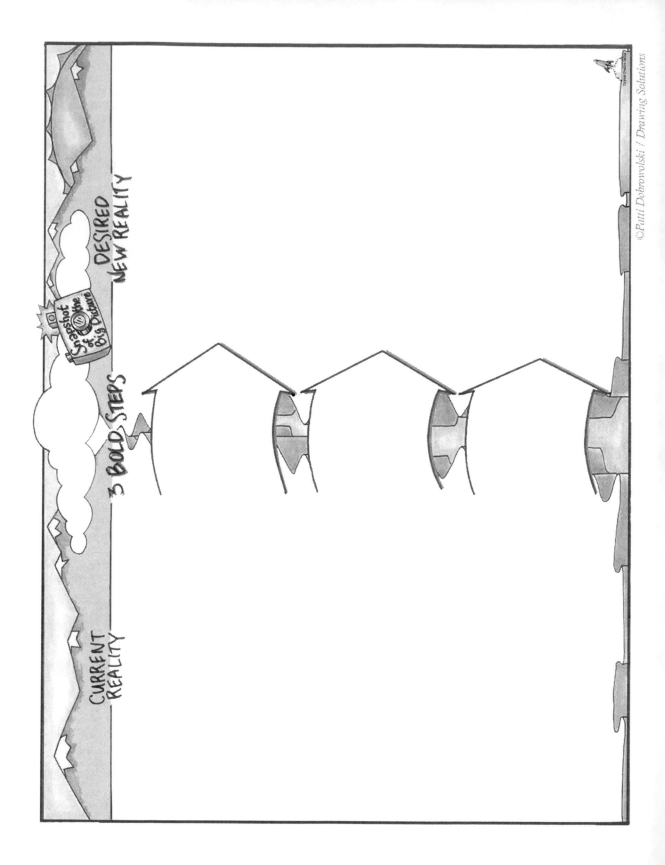

CURRENT REALITY: ASSESSING YOUR LIFE

On the previous page is a template for the Snapshot of the Big Picture process. You can use this, or the **Quick Guide to Mapping** in Section Four, which follows the sequence of as we go along. You can also download the template free on my website at **www.upyourcreativegenius.com/snapshottemplate.**[1] Earmark or pull the template out of your book, as it will be easier for you to work with. I suggest you clear out a space on a desk or table so you have plenty of room, and remove any distractions.[2] You will also want some colored pencils or pens. Don't let finding the perfect workstation or supplies distract you from getting started; dig up a box of crayons or a couple of highlighters for the places where I ask you to "color." This entire mapping process (Current, Desired, Bold Steps) will take anywhere from forty-five minutes to ninety minutes to complete, depending upon your pace.

Exercise: Draw Your Current Reality

First things first: write your name in that center cloud at the top of the map. Then color all around your name with your favorite color. For those of you groaning at the fact that I just asked you to color, here's a brain fact: when you draw with color, you actually send a message to the critical, left side of your brain to relax, and one to your right side to activate and be open.[3]

In this exercise, you can choose to examine a singular aspect of your life that you want to adjust, or you can use this map to get an overview of the bigger picture of how things are going in your life. By creating a visual record of the big picture with both words and images, you can easily pinpoint the things you need to change right now. Once you have decided which aspect of your life to focus on, it is time to assess what it looks and feels like to be you at this moment. All of this should be captured on the Current Reality side of your map.

Reflect on where you are in this moment: what's going well in your world, as well as what is currently challenging you. Be completely honest. Don't waste your time trying to talk yourself out of your feelings about parts of your life that aren't working for you. Even if you have no idea about what to do to change these things, include them on your map. Strategies for getting from here to there will come later.

Your goal in the first part of this exercise is to capture the essence of your thoughts and feelings using single words. Scatter your words around the Current Reality side of the page any way you like. However, it is important not to make neat lists or impose any kind of order on the words you write. This breaks up the patterning your left hemisphere naturally reverts to when you create a list. Your left side of the brain loves routine, so your job is to signal that you are embarking on a new way of doing things. By emphasizing this, which is what you do when you scatter your words randomly, you speed up your ability to access new ideas, thoughts and feelings.

Be sure to keep your writing small enough that you have room to add images in the next part of this exercise. You may have to condense your thoughts/feelings into simple words or concepts so you don't run out of room. For example instead of writing "I am feeling stuck" just write "stuck."

Here are some questions to help you:

- *What does it feel like to be living my life right now?* Examples of words others have used to answer this question include: confused, bored, love my work but not my boss, in a dead-end job...

- *What am I doing now (or what have I been doing until now)?* This is where you come up with a specific description of not only what you actually do (or did), for example, "stay-at-home Mom," along with the associated tasks such as "manage household," "run the PTA"...

- *What are my finances like right now?* How much money am I making? Am I satisfied with my income? Be sure to capture specific qualities and characteristics of how you feel: happy, disappointed, worried, scared, satisfied, excited, elated or depressed...

- *What is the state of my relationships?* Do I feel I have the love and support I need from my partner, spouse, family, and friends?

- *What is the state of my spiritual life?* Does my spiritual practice/life have a place in my daily life? Does it meet my needs for meaning in my life?

- *What is the state of my health?* Am I happy with my physical body or do I feel I need to make changes? Am I getting enough exercise? Enough sleep? Am I eating the kinds of foods that I know are good for me?

Write a word or short phrase to describe the qualities and characteristics of your Current Reality. Keep in mind that you are creating a snapshot of your life at this moment. Let it all out! Whatever you are experiencing right now, good and bad. Then, when your pens have come to a standstill, take a step back and look over the Current Reality of you. Is anything missing?

Now, add some images.

By drawing images to go with the words, you are integrating both sides of your brain. The quality of what you draw is not important. Your drawings, no matter what they look like, are communicating a powerful message to the right side of your brain. This is the side we need to activate. This sets you up to move on to the second part of this process – creating a Desired New Reality. In the Appendix you will find a few image ideas if you get stuck. Feel free to trace them right into your map.

So start adding pictures that represent the words you have written on your map. If you wrote 'stuck', you might end up drawing a person pinned to the page, a guy trapped in a cave, a stop sign or a person standing at the edge of a cliff. It is important to leave

enough space to capture all of the important thoughts and feelings you are experiencing using both words and images. Remember what I said about the visual and how it helps both sides of your brain integrate. And remember the emotionality about what you are thinking and feeling.

Be sure you are only including what you *are* experiencing, not what you *wish you were* experiencing. We'll get to that later.

TAKE A CLOSER LOOK

Look at the Current Reality side of your Snapshot map. Try to take in all the aspects of your Current Reality from a different perspective, one layer down. Go back and bring into your map the Unsaids from the previous chapter. Is there an underlying pattern in what you have written and drawn? Add some of your Unsaids to your Current Reality.

Can you identify anything that has been getting in your way of making changes in your world? What obstacles or behaviors have you encountered? Here are some examples of how this might look:

THOUGHT	FEELING
I just took this job, how can I quit already?	Guilt
I've got a family to feed. I can't start my own business.	Fear
No matter how much I exercise, I never lose weight.	Lack of conviction

There are often beliefs or behaviors that block us from making changes. Can you identify any current challenges that may be acting as obstacles in your life? If so, take a minute now to capture them on your map. I sometimes draw a few rock-like shapes around those obstacles. If you don't have enough room to write words, draw a few more symbols.

How does the Current Reality side of your map look now? It is probably a little messy. Relax your focus. What patterns do you see there? By allowing patterns to emerge, we warm up the parts of our brain that generate deeper insights into our lives. This capitalizes on the visual processing aspect that Dan Roam describes in *The Back of the Napkin*. Without judgment, look at all the words and images on the left side of your map. What do you see there? Suspend your left-brain criticism (you know, that voice that is still stuck on how childlike your drawings look), and get curious about what you have created.

- What jumps out at you from that Current Reality? Any surprises?

- What looks familiar?

- What patterns do you see?

- Do particular images have lots of energy or feeling for you?

- Which things in your Current Reality are you doing well right now?

- Circle or draw a star next to things that seem to form patterns.

You might want to add a clarifying note either directly on your template or on a separate piece of paper. The map is a way to get an overall picture of your life and to pinpoint, in images, what is and isn't working.

Now, as we prepare to step into your future, I suggest you pour yourself an eight-ounce glass of water and drink it slowly and consciously. Drinking water rejuvenates your energy after about 30 seconds.[4] Then, take a deep breath, do a short meditation. Or run around your house or yard a few times as fast as possible. Or put on the most inspirational song you know and sing along with it at the top of your lungs. Do something different that signals your mind that you are about to shift from the left side of your brain (the part that helps to keep you safe), into the right side of your brain (the part that knows anything and everything is possible).

CREATING YOUR DESIRED NEW REALITY

Once your have done something to shift out of your typical, everyday routine, look at your Snapshot template again.

Exercise: Creating Your Desired New Reality

This time put your focus on the blank right side of your template, the Desired New Reality. Now close your eyes and begin to dream.

Ask yourself, "In the best-case scenario, if all goes well and everything works out just perfectly, what will my life look and feel like one year from today? What new qualities and characteristics will I be experiencing?"

Now let your mind wander into that fantastic new reality. It might start off slowly as you tune out the sounds in your immediate environment. As soon as you get some ideas about what you want to be experiencing one year from today, even if they are vague at first, write them down on the right side of your map as quickly as you can. Remember the "Exploring Your Options" exercise where you asked what you should be doing next? Here is where you add some of those insights as well.

Try to capture the insights and ideas that come to you within the first few seconds, before they are overridden by other thoughts that may limit or censor your dreaming. As you did when you filled in the Current Reality side of the map, write words and draw pictures of what you see or imagine in your mind's eye. Remember, you are picturing the *best-case scenario*. You don't have to have any ideas or plans about how to make these images within reality.[5]

Remain in this positive frame of mind as long as you can, allowing all of the ideas or images to emerge into your consciousness. Take as long  as you need to expand upon and capture all aspects of your dream. Do you want more abundance? Draw a stack of hundred-dollar bills.

Do you desire more love? Draw a picture of a heart or a house with a family standing by it.

Are you longing for more freedom? Sketch an open door. Remember to continue to relax about how your drawings look; if your inner critical voice inside needs reassurance, remind yourself that drawing activates both sides of the brain and paves the way for new ideas to enter.

The images you capture on your map should be very personal and relevant. For some people, the specific images of their Desired New Reality are very concrete. I remember someone in one of my workshops who wanted a BMW 3-Series car, and not long afterward ending up owning one.

However, sometimes the changes we want to see are more complex. I once attended a workshop led by Mary Carroll Moore, author of *How to Master Change in Your Life*. She suggested focusing on only the qualities and characteristics you wanted to have in the future. She reassured us that life would take care of how you acquired those qualities.

In my own experience, I have seen Desired New Realities manifest in both ways. I have put an image on a dream board and seen the exact image show up in my life. And I have also asked for qualities I wanted to possess, and life has brought the necessary experiences to transform me from a lump of coal into something more polished.

What qualities do you want to have by this time next year? Creativity? Freedom? Abundance? Fun?

In addition to words and images, add auditory signals to your Desired New Reality. This is especially important if you are not a person who thinks in pictures. When some people imagine things, they may get more of a feeling in their body (kinesthetic), or hear an imaginary conversation (auditory) describing that future. Ask yourself, "What will people be saying to me a year from today?" You might draw a few cartoon bubbles and describe what your friends, co-workers, or even the press will be saying to you or about you. What will you be saying to yourself? How might you feel inside? Capture your own words of acknowledgment or gratitude for what you will have accomplished at that future date.

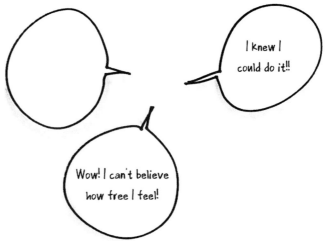

When you have put as many of the things you desire as you can think of on the right side of your map, step back and look at what you have imagined. Add color to your pictures or pictures to your words. If you have written anything that includes the word "no,"[6] change what you have written into a positive statement describing what you do want to see. For example, if you wrote "no stress," you might substitute "work-life balance."

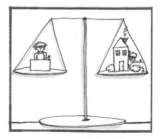

The mind cannot distinguish "no" so it will focus on whatever you have written or drawn on that right side of the map. A good example of this is when you say to a child, "Now, don't go near the pool!" What will they remember? "There's a pool! They have a pool!" The mind only remembers the image, not the "don't."

Once you have looked over your map to be sure you have captured positive statements and images, then continue to simply absorb your Desired New Reality.

Expand your fantasy a little further and imagine yourself having all of the aspects of that reality. Imagine waking up into that world. Feel it as fully as possible. Close your eyes and imagine all the big and little details. By allowing yourself to fully "feel" this experience as if you are on the inside of it looking out, you are imprinting your long-term memory with these images.[7] Your drawings are a simple reminder of what you want. But the feeling, the attention and love, what you hear and how it makes you feel—that's what creates the magnetic pull that brings those things to you.

Psych-K,[8] a powerful method for changing your beliefs as a way of changing your life, encourages adding all three components to your vision of the future: visual, auditory and kinesthetic. This combination helps the subconscious lock the desired future outcome into memory. In fact, the more time and energy you spend locking in a multi-dimensional experience of what you desire, as if it is happening right now, the stronger the signal you send out to magnetize this new reality.[9] This simple technique has the power to overcome obstacles in your subconscious.

In the process of creating your Snapshot of the Big Picture, you are making a personal map that you will want to return to again and again to remind your conscious (and subconscious) mind of where and who you are now. Once you have created this image, you have initiated the process of change; it is as simple as that.

Here's how one of my workshop participants explained her mapping process:

"The process helped pull various elements I was already aware of into a complete picture. In the end, it was so helpful to see the relationships among them all. Creating a literal picture helped me to better understand how all of the elements were connected. As a result, I felt more astute and confident in taking risks."

~Linda Knutsen McAusland

THREE BOLD STEPS TO GET RESULTS

Great job! The map in front of you now gives you a clear picture of where you are, your Current Reality, and where you desire to be one year from today, your Desired New Reality. Your next task is one that the left side of your brain can really sink its teeth into: crossing the bridges of the Bold Steps and doing something!

The process I am recommending requires you to come up with not one but *three* Bold Steps, which can be daunting. We all make minor changes every day, but when you really want to make a solid, positive shift in a new direction, you have to take big BOLD steps, not just make a little tactical adjustment. Bold is much more than just rearranging your file cabinets. A Bold Step is usually so big that you may need to take a bunch of smaller steps to achieve it.

This is the point where some people freeze up. They can't think of a way to get from the left side, where they are now, to the right side, what they desire. Why does this happen? Because, if you have been completely honest, you are beginning to realize that many of the things you desire, on the right side, will require you to step out of your comfort zone. This idea is terrifying for the left side of your brain because it prefers to do the same things over and over.

To make matters worse, it is at this point that the voice of your inner critic (who has been patiently waiting in the wings for an opportunity to drum some sense into you) begins to weigh in. You know that voice. It is the one who says things like:

"You don't know how to get from here to there. If you did, you would have already done it!" Or "Ha! Just wait until you show this to (fill in the blank); are they ever gonna laugh at you!" Or "It takes more than a pretty map to solve your problems, you are in a mess!" Say you put something on the right side of your map that you've never done before, and find it difficult to believe you will know how to get there. In my twenty years of

using this process, I have found no matter what you need to change, you really DO know what to do, even though you don't know the exact path to take.

It is important to keep reminding yourself of this: when you really want to make a change, you must *change the pattern* by approaching the process of change in a new way. For example, if you want to lose weight, it is not enough to simply stop eating; you have to *change your lifestyle as well as the things you eat*. If you dump your lover for the same reasons you dumped your last four, going in search of someone new will not result in someone better, because … well you know how that story ends! Repeating the same strategies produces the same outcomes.

Exercise: Three Bold Steps

Look at the Desired New Reality you successfully created on your map. Reassure yourself that you also have what you need to create the bridges to reach it. Take a deep breath and bring your conscious mind fully into the present moment. Allow the past to fade,

taking with it any failures. Your conscious mind has two options: being in the present, where change is possible; or being in the past, where worry and regret keep you from changing.

Let's get ready to create your Bold Steps. You may want to just start writing something as a way of unlocking your frozen brain. Get a piece of scratch paper and start brainstorming ideas without worrying about how bold they are. If at any point you feel overwhelmed, close your eyes to block out any outside stimulation, take a few deep breaths, and ask the wisest part of yourself, "What are the three boldest things I can do right now to bring myself from my Current Reality to my Desired New Reality?" As you begin to get insights, immediately capture them on your paper.

Give yourself ample time to let every idea emerge. When you feel complete, review your list of possible steps. Do any of them scare you? If so, that's a good indicator that they are BOLD. Will any of them stretch you? Are there any that would require small steps to achieve the bigger and bolder one? If any step seems easy or effortless, eliminate it or spend some time rewriting it to make it bolder.

Some examples of other people's Bold Steps are:

Highlight the Bold Steps on your list that you think have potential. Then work on them to make them short and sweet. It's critical that they make sense to you, and it is even better if they inspire or scare you a little (or a lot!) when you see them. One of the women for whom I did a mapping session, Susie, is a non-stop go-getter. She runs her own business, has adopted two Vietnamese children who lost limbs when a land mine exploded, and is positive and inspirational. She came to me because she felt "stuck." She didn't know why, but when her long-term client contract ended, she just couldn't get a move on. Her Current Reality was filled with lots of home-related projects and kid-related activities. Her Desired

New Reality was populated with words like "work that I love, abundance, job aligned with who I am and what I do best." When it came to crafting her Bold Steps she froze. She said, "I know I should know how to get from here to there, but really I'm so afraid. I know I shouldn't be, but I am." I suggested we write BE BRAVE as one of her Bold Steps. "Yes!" she said emphatically. The other two Bold Steps just came right out. Here is what she wrote me afterwards:

> *"The key to achieving my future was not any "thing" but by "being" courageous. I flexed and stretched my courageous muscles over and over again and overcame my paralysis and obstacles that were causing conversations and stories in my head."*
>
> *~ Susie Cantor*

I find that clients' Three Bold Steps tend to fall into three categories:

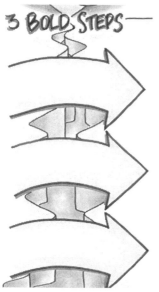

• One of those Bold Steps is usually the big one they have been keeping inside, like "Quit my job," "Leave this relation-ship" or "Stop smoking." This first step is usually simple, though requiring some pretty big changes, and is often the first thing that comes to mind.

• A second Bold Step tends to require a change to their immediate environment, like "Talk to my family and make a plan," "Create a better work environment" or ""Get serious about my health."

• And the third Bold Step is often self-reflective, tapping into the more personal dimensions of change, something like "Believe in myself," "Be more present," or "Step outside my comfort zone."

While some clients create those Bold Steps in that order, for other people like Susie, that BE BRAVE Bold Step unlocked her ability to think through her next two Bold Steps.

You will know your steps are right if they enerize you, even if at first glance they are daunting. When I am working with clients, once they have come up with their Bold Steps, I hear them say *That feels right! This is exactly what I need to do!* No matter how competent a change agent you are, when it comes to really committing to have the life, or job, or relationship you dream about, you should expect it to shake you up a bit. Quoted in *Chicken Soup for the Soul*, Alan Cohen writes, *"It takes a lot of courage to release the familiar and seemingly secure, to embrace the new. But there is no real security in what is no longer meaningful. There is more security in the adventurous and exciting, for in movement there is life, and in change there is power."*[10]

There is no better time than now to shake things up!

When you have worked with your Three Bold Steps so that they are simple and somewhat challenging, write them on your map, one step per arrow.

You now have the basic elements of your change plan. See if you can shift your mindset from looking at what is on the left side of your map to *living* the right side, because now it's real. Not only have you said what you dreamed out loud, you've written it down. Yikes! You drew pictures of it! Not only did you write down what you wanted, you wrote down what you have to do to access the life you desire.

You should feel both a sense of relief and excitement, and maybe even a few butterflies in your stomach! Sit back and look at what you have created. This is your plan and your vision. No matter how long it takes to make it real, it *will* happen. It is possible that every little thing may not turn out exactly as you imagined it, but the things that you really want most certainly will become real. It's only a matter of time and trust.

Here's how it worked for Pam:

"Six years ago I created a Snapshot of the Big Picture map in a session with Patti. The process allowed me to mark a moment in time and to clearly establish where I was and where I wanted to go. Now, when I review my map, I can see that when I detailed my Current Reality, I listed a bunch of facts that described me. Whereas my Desired New Reality was more global, grand and inspirational. I imagined work with meaning, an opportunity to be successful, and most of all, to know why I'm in this world, my purpose. I believed I would arrive at a place when people would know me and my reputation so that I would never have to "apply" for work again.

When I was hired for my current position, I was recruited because my work was well known. There were no other candidates. The Board of Directors reviewed my résumé (with my name blacked out), and yet they all knew me. I was hired. I now realize that my current work is where I've been headed all along."

Pamela Harris, President & CEO
Mile High Montessori Early Learning Centers

Exercise: Action Steps

Look back at your big Bold Steps and begin to break them down into small, manageable actions. This activity should take you about thirty minutes. In the space provided, or on the worksheet at the back of this book, write each Bold Step that you have on your map.

Beneath each one, list all of the small steps you believe you will have to take in order to accomplish it. Don't worry about the order you put them in right now, just brainstorm as many actions as you can. If Bold Step #1 is "Quit My Job," one of the action steps might be "Have a conversation with my family to let them know that I am not happy working where I am," or "Let my family know that I plan to finally quit." Another action step might be, "Start saving money for a change," or "Figure out what else I can do by going to informational interviews with people in fields I am interested in."

BOLD STEP 1:   **BOLD STEP 2:**   **BOLD STEP 3:**

Try to come up with about ten small actions under each of your Bold Steps. It's okay to have fewer than ten actions, just be sure not to rush through the brainstorming process. Now apply the 80/20 Rule, which says that on a list of ten things, two of them produce about an 80 percent return on your investment of time. The remaining eight will net you about a 20 percent return. Time is a precious thing, so look at your list and pick the top two actions on each list that are going to result in the biggest bang for your buck. Note them as the things you want to act on first.

At this point you should have six actions that stand out: two key actions per Bold Step. These are the actions you start working on from this moment forward and into the next week. Now you are creating your Action Plan. It must work for you, so if these actions still seem too big to implement immediately, try breaking them down into smaller, bite-size pieces.

Write your first steps down on paper and carry them with you. You might also put them on your calendar, on your computer as your screen saver, on your bathroom mirror, or any place where you can see and review them often. This visual reminder of your strategy will help prioritize your actions and keep you focused. Think of your plan as your security blanket. It will reassure you anytime you doubt your new direction. If your inner critic starts up, your plan is proof that you really do know what you are doing—and you do!

USE A MINI-MAP TO HELP SHIFT YOUR PERSPECTIVE

When you are in the midst of big life changes, it sometimes feels that your life as you knew it is falling apart and you are losing your sense of direction. You think you know where you are headed until something unexpected happens. Or so many opportunities are coming at you, you don't know what to do next. Later, you think, "Wow! I really made such a big deal out of that (losing my job, ending a relationship, physical challenges, and so on). Now I see that all of it had to happen to get me to this great … (new job, partner, you name it)." What makes the actual change process so overwhelming, even if you ultimately end up in a better place, is that along the way you were unable to step back and see the whole pattern as it emerged. What you need to navigate big changes is a way to stay aligned with your own True North.[11]

While a map of the bigger changes you want to make (generally done once a year) is great for charting individual or business growth, you may also create a Mini-Map, as I used with the person sitting next to me on the plane ride. The Mini-Map will help you gain perspective on one or more pieces of the larger map of your life.

Let's say one goal in your New Desired Reality is to adopt a healthier lifestyle. A Mini-Map will help you honestly assess the Current State of your health. For example, you could draw a picture of yourself holding a bunch of medicine bottles with a big swollen belly to depict frequent bouts of indigestion, or draw yourself dozing in a recliner with a TV remote to show your lack of energy.

On the Desired New Reality side of your Mini-Map, you might create images of yourself playing tennis, wearing a svelte outfit that shows off your great muscles, or an empty medicine chest.

Remember, you don't have to know how you are going to get from where you are now to where you desire to be. You only have to honestly assess where you are and then visualize what you want to see happen. Next on the Mini-Map, outline specific steps that will both contribute to and be a part of your success. Here you are filling in your Bold Steps and adding Action Steps, but all in the context of only one desired goal from your bigger map. Continue through all the steps for creating your action plan. Refer to the **Quick Guide to Mapping** in Section Four. Be sure to add action steps to your daily calendar to track the progress. This enables the Mini-Map to keep you focused on your goal each day, while it re-inspires you and kick-starts that good brain chemistry.

While you might spend a longer time putting together your initial Snapshot Map, a Mini-Map is something you create quickly and use to plan out a small project or to illuminate one aspect of a Snapshot Map. It can be as simple or complex as you want. Use a Mini-Map anytime you need to charge up your energy and motivation for your big-picture tasks. It will help you mark progress, unearth truth and solidify your desire to successfully reach your goals.

Now you have your map in hand or on the wall. Great job! Now you have a roadmap, so take a deep breath and relax. Have a cup of coffee, a bite to eat or a well-deserved nap. Your map is already working for you—your brain is busy adjusting the priorities of your reward system based on that Desired New Reality. Now that you have set yourself up for success, I'll show you how to maximize the work you've completed.

PART THREE

WORKING WITH VISUAL MAPS: WHAT TO EXPECT ALONG THE WAY

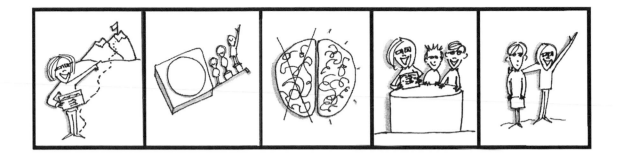

Congratulations on completing your Snapshot map! You will quickly discover it is a powerful tool for setting and achieving life goals. As you embark on your journey, here are some guidelines for understanding the road ahead and navigating any challenges.

CLARIFY YOUR EXPECTATIONS

It's important to set clear expectations for your goals. This is also known as getting yourself aligned. What do you expect from these Bold Steps? How do you expect your performance to improve? How will you recognize when you have achieved your Desired Reality goals? Clear goals not only keep you motivated, they are your yardstick for success.

When I turned 50, I made a list of 50 new things I wanted to do. I did this both to challenge myself and to experiment with parts of myself that I didn't know much about. One of my goals was to ride one stage of the Tour de France bike race course. I wasn't planning to ride with the professional bike teams, but rather, to ride the stage during the following summer.

Since an average Tour de France stage is about 120 miles long, I would need to be in excellent physical shape. To develop a logical action plan, I consulted biking friends. Following one friend's suggestion, I researched and joined a local women's "Meet the Teams" ride, and headed out on bike for my first group ride. It was exactly twenty-five miles. Despite having only ridden a maximum of twenty miles previously, and encountering dark moments of doubt along the way, I made it to the end with the rest of the women!

Encouraged, I rode with several other teams until I found one that I really liked. Joining a bike team was the beginning of an amazing experience that revealed parts of myself I never knew existed.

Bike racers are very committed. In fall and winter they typically meet early every Saturday and Sunday morning for a two-to-four hour ride. This happens even in the pouring rain, which is a common occurrence in the Pacific Northwest. When ice and snow make outdoor rides impossible, we ride indoors for hours. After four months of training with the team, I could hardly WAIT for the racing season to start. Once it did, something strange and surprising happened. I suddenly became as competitive and wild as a 16-year-old boy, determined to do whatever was needed to be the first biker across the finish line. I turned into someone I didn't recognize, someone completely obsessed with bike racing. All I could think or talk about was racing. I even created my own Mini-Map just about racing.

At the beginning of the season, I set a goal to finish in the top ten in a race in my category, CAT 4 Women. The one event that I particularly liked was the time trial (TT). The time trial is called the "race of truth" because it is just you racing against the clock. You ride a specified distance as fast as possible. The very first race in Seattle took place in February, when most Seattleites were in Hawaii, because having lived through the dreariness of four months of constant rain deserved a reward.

I, however, was not on vacation because I was a bike racer! I decided that the first event, the Frostbite TT, would be my first race of the season. Prior to my start time, I did

all the necessary preparations: got warmed up by riding my bike on a trainer outside in the pouring rain; ate and drank the right amounts of proteins and carbs, then an energy gel just before the race to raise my glucose level, and half a bottle of water for hydration. The race began, and boom, I was off! The ride was incredibly difficult: in February with brutal rain and wind, I could barely see. But during the race, I actually passed someone else who started 30 seconds ahead of me! When I got to the finish line I was elated, and drove home singing a happy little song. Later when I checked the results online, my stomach dropped; my finish time put me second to last.

What was I missing? My goal was to "be a successful bike racer," but when I looked at my map I saw my definitions weren't clear. What did "successful" mean? Now that I knew I could come in second to last, where did I want to see myself next? Top ten! I added that to my map. Now I knew I was going to have to study time trial racing. I added another action to my map: using Internet searches to help me

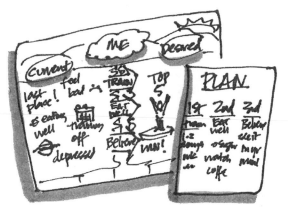

understand what my speed must be to beat the record. My research showed me that the best time in my race category was set by someone racing an average speed of 17 mph. If I increased my speed to 17 mph or above, I might just beat my opponents. I kept training hard. At the next race, I finished in 8th place! Top ten finish! I did it!

Just as positive expectations and a clear intent were keys to my success, they will be to yours as well. Sometimes that intent changes, as you discover exactly what it takes to reach your goal. When I clarified my definition by stating my intent to place in the top ten when bike-racing, and I did everything I could to prepare myself to meet my expectations, I was one step closer to my larger goal for my 50th year, riding one stage in the Tour de France. And because my Mini-Map documented my processes, it helped me use my first race finish as the catalyst for a clearer action plan.

Exercise: Intent and Clarification

Take some time now to look at your map and your Desired New Reality. To achieve the goals depicted there, what must change? What do you expect from yourself in terms of specific actions that will bring you closer to your goals?

- My intent for change for Bold Step #1:

- My intent for change for Bold Step #2:

- My intent for change for Bold Step #3:

Once you have stated your intent and clarified your expectations, you are ready to follow through on the action steps for your plan. These are the ten (or fewer) actions that you listed and then, using the 80/20 Rule, narrowed down to the top two.

When I realized that the women who had won previous races had ridden at a certain speed, I knew I had to match or exceed it to reach my goal of finishing in the top ten. I had refined my actions to a specific goal.

After prioritizing your actions and clarifying your goals, take the steps necessary to prepare for success. And always express your expectations as "this, or something better" which leaves room for the unexpected to manifest.

By doing all this, it is as if you have put up an invisible but powerful barrier—one that will protect you from the minefield of doubts you are likely to encounter on the road ahead. The picture in your mind is constantly evolving, and plays a big part in your ability to circumvent or resolve issues when they arise. You can evolve your image by approaching it from different perspectives. Your imagination and creativity will reboot your enthusiasm and your belief that you will succeed.

For example, imagine yourself viewing the map as if you were someone else. To get new ideas, I imagine I am one of those mentors who taught me key lessons. I might pretend I am Michael, who helped me kick-start my financial planning. What would Michael add to this picture or my action plan?

Another way to solidify your process is to write a contract with yourself that states, "I will do everything in my power to bring this plan to fruition." Then, sign and date the document and mail a copy to yourself or someone who also believes in your dream.

In group visioning and strategy sessions, I often ask participants to sign their names to the bottom of the map we have created. Somewhere in our genetic encoding we know that when we sign our name to something, we believe it will happen and we commit ourselves to making it so.

Those Bold Steps require us to dig deep into the suitcase for the courage to get what we want. The Desired New Reality creates a pull, while our discomfort with the Current Reality provides the push. Then our commitment and dedication to the action plan creates a momentum that carries us over the Bold Step bridges into the world of our dreams.

SET SUCCESS MEASURES

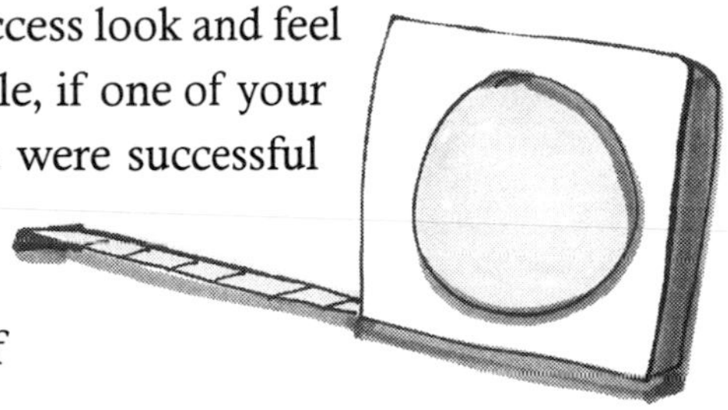

How can you measure change success? What will success look and feel like when you have taken that Bold Step? For example, if one of your Bold Steps is to quit your job, you might know you were successful when you find yourself in a new job you completely love. If another Bold Step is a deeper relationship with your spiritual self, success might be a feeling of inner peace.

Exercise: Success Measures

For each of your Bold Steps, imagine what it will look and feel like when you have stepped across that chasm into your Desired New Reality. Write it down right now.

Bold Step 1:

Success Measure:

-
-
-

Bold Step 2:

Success Measure:

-
-
-

Bold Step 3:

Success Measure:

-
-
-

REVISIT YOUR MAP REGULARLY

Remember my friend Michael helping me envision a higher income? When I first stated that I wanted to achieve that increased income he had me break it down by quarter, by month, then by week. Together we looked at what resources, options and unique strategies I could activate to make that amount of money. We identified how much would come from my gardening business, drama therapy groups and corporate consulting clients. Each week I would review my calendar. There, I tracked my income (actual and potential), client contacts, and any actions I had taken towards my goals. One day my friend Nancy joked, "When I want to relax, I go take a nap or a bath; when Patti relaxes she looks at her calendar." Funny, but oh so true! For me, revisiting my plans showed me I was making progress and kept my energy high.

Exercise: Reviewing Your Map and Checklist

Set aside some time to review your map and refresh your checklist of small manageable actions. Ask yourself, what have I completed on my list? How was I successful in shifting toward my new direction? What changes in my attitude have I noticed? Allow ample time to look at your progress from every angle.

Next make a new list of ten things under each Bold Step. You might add some of the things from last week's list that you weren't able to get to. If you "never seem to get to" a couple of items, these things are not really the priority. Replace them with something else. By keeping them there, you just disperse your energy by worrying about your ability to follow through or by making up excuses about why you didn't get it done. The left side of your brain is simply programmed to "get to the bottom of things" and if given free will, it does its job of pulling you down that slippery slope into the treacherous explanation, "I'm not good enough." Help your mind come back into the present by creating action steps that you can *get behind* and you will find you have plenty of energy to do those new things.

Now that you have a new list of ten things, just like before, choose two "big bang for your buck" items to put your attention on. These six things will be what you work on right away to help you across those bridges.

While working to increase my annual income, reviewing my calendar also helped me determine if I needed to step up my efforts. For example, if I didn't have enough clients and projects lined up to make my monthly monetary goal, I would make time to call all my potential clients to see how their businesses were doing, or I'd spend an hour or more contacting my network of friends, colleagues or anyone who might have a potential work lead to remind them of my availability. My calendar acted as a road map, grounding rod, and motivator.

My clients report they achieve their visions more quickly, when they make time regularly to do what I call "keeping their map alive." This involves spending time looking at the images on their maps—what they desire—and then allowing themselves the time to imagine, or daydream about, what they want to see happen. Many put their maps in a prominent place in their home or office where they can contemplate their plan each day.

Some years ago I worked with Chris, a woman about to leave her job as vice president of human resources for a Fortune 500 company. She planned to use the generous severance pay to tide her over while she started her own consulting practice. When we first met, she had already taken some steps toward starting her business. We used the name she had in mind for her company to inspire her map. Normally I would write the company name at the top center of the map (in this instance, a 4' x 8' map). But because I knew Chris was an expansive person, I wrote the title stretching across the top of the paper in a calligraphic style, then repeated it in lighter colors along the top. That set the tone.

She was an inspired participant and honestly spoke to the fear and excitement she was experiencing in her Current Reality, embarking on this new adventure. She had recently become interested in Buddhism and had begun a daily practice that included yoga and meditation. Chris felt her deepening spiritual practice would help her work through any fears that emerged. Her Desired New Reality was filled with lots of possibilities, things she had been dreaming about for years, but had not acted on due to her very intense and time-consuming corporate job. She carefully chose her three Bold Steps and we set her up with an immediate action plan.

On the way out the door, Chris promised to do everything in her power to make that dream happen. Less than six months later she called: "I have to schedule another session with you to do a new map! I already did everything on that old one!" She truly was like a rocket ship blasting out of my office!

CELEBRATE

When you start a new venture, like a new business or job, you may feel doubts and wonder, "Can I really take care of myself?" "Will I have enough money to survive?" "Have I made a terrible mistake?" Your critical mind needs lots of reassurance because all of this is new, and "new" can mean "bad" to the part of you that thrives on routine.

It is important to stay calm despite your fear. One great way I've found to rewire my brain in a new direction is to celebrate the small stuff. I was creating a vision with a mountain-climbing theme for a shipping company, and Kit DesLaurier was the keynote speaker. She was the first woman to ski down Mt. Everest—and the first person to ski down all the highest peaks in the world. In her talk, she showed an amazing video of herself putting on her skis at the top and carefully making her way down the sheer face, where to fall would mean certain death. I asked her afterward, "How did you do that? How did you keep from being afraid?" She said, "I set small goals. I would say to myself, 'If I can just ski to that bump right there.' And when I got there, I would say, 'I made it! Now, can I get to that dark shadowy place over there?' And by setting one small goal at a time I eventually made it down the mountain." Achieving small goals builds your confidence.

Success is just a series of small steps coupled together. You earn small wins by completing each of your ten Action Steps; this helps reassure you that you can succeed as you move toward your Bold Steps. Kit acknowledged her small successes. When you do, your sense of yourself will shift and you'll start reminding yourself that you are someone who can and does succeed.

Tom Bird, a very successful author and writing coach, encourages his clients to reinforce their subconscious by doing something as simple as raising a coffee cup or a glass of water and saying aloud, "I drink this coffee/

water/wine in celebration of finishing this chapter!" Tom believes that acknowledgement reprograms the brain to want to do more—in this case, writing. Repeated acknowledgment sustains your enthusiasm for what may sometimes be a challenging process.

Be sure to celebrate and acknowledge yourself for each small (or large) task you have completed. Stop everything and give yourself a little pep talk. Tell yourself: "I did it! Things are changing! This is the right direction! Things are good."

After you celebrate, take a moment to be grateful. Gratitude keeps the cycle of manifestation continuing: you ask, you receive, and you give thanks.

After one of my clients or teams completes a Snapshot of the Big Picture map, we do exercises to fire up their imagination and visualize the goals as already being part of their world. This accelerates the changes that will take them there. Now it's your turn to envision the future as a waking dream happening right now. You do that by living it as fully as possible, in this moment—and by enhancing that vision in your mind's eye until it manifests.

Exercise: Wake Up to Your Dream

One technique is to wake up in the morning behaving as if your New Desired Reality is already happening. Spend five or ten minutes imaging yourself moving through your

entire day with that belief. Your imagination can lead you to discover things about your dream that were not apparent at first. Use your imagination like a matrix, to initiate a pattern that you can revisit later to discover what's new or changed. Think of your imagination as the vehicle that carries your visions from your subconscious, or subtle, mind to your conscious mind. When you visualize, you are actually using your imagination to help you create the picture. Allow the picture to become more expansive. Like a scene in a movie that continues to unfold, you begin to build a story of that Desired New Reality. The story helps your brain remember—and the more positive and colorful the story is, the stronger the memory becomes.

VISUALIZATION

See how this all works by taking about fifteen minutes for this easy and powerful visualization. (you may also listen to this by downloading a Podcast, at: www.upyourcreativegenius.com/visualization.

Exercise: Visualization

You'll need a copy of your Snapshot, a pen, some paper, and a quiet place where you won't be disturbed by other people or electronics. Have paper and pen handy to write down your experience. Start by taking a good look at your Snapshot of the Big Picture map. Then focus on the words and images under the Desired New Reality. Close your eyes and take a few deep breaths to bring yourself into this present moment. Relax any part of your body that is feeling tense. Ready?

Imagine yourself getting into an elevator. As you step inside, notice what kind of elevator you are in, what the interior looks like, and if it has a particular smell or feeling. The smell and feeling part helps you better access other senses if you are not necessarily a visual person.

Now push the button for floor 5. Imagine each breath taking you and the elevator one floor higher. You entered the elevator at ground 0, so your first breath takes you up to floor 1. Imagine the lighting panel illuminating "1" as you pass floor 1. Exhale, then inhale deeply as you pass floor 2. Continue to inhale and exhale as you see the lights on the elevator buttons go to 3, 4 and finally 5, where the elevator stops. You have arrived.

The elevator doors slide open to reveal a field of rolling hills covered with tall beautiful grass swaying in the wind. Step out into the field. Notice the time of day. What does the air feel or smell like? Notice any sounds you hear around you. After you have taken in your surroundings, begin to move through the grass toward the hills you can see in the distance. Notice how effortless it is to move through the field; you are just gliding along.

As you get closer to the hills, you begin to feel excited—that fluttery sensation you get when you are about to see or do something surprising and new: pure anticipation. Let this feeling of positive expectation build as you move closer and closer to the hills.

When you arrive at the base of the first hill, begin to climb up the hillside, taking note of the terrain. Is it rocky, or grassy? Are you walking or climbing? Is it steep or gradual?

As you climb, continue to feel your growing anticipation for whatever awaits you at the top. Somehow you know that when you reach the top you are going to see something fantastic that has to do with your *vision of the future*.

Continue your climb. Take as long as you need to reach the top. When you arrive, take a few deep breaths and look into the valley that lies just beyond. As you gaze into the valley, you realize that what you see before you is your desired future in the form of a structure of some kind. The structure might appear as a complete building, or it may be just the foundation or a building in progress. (Or perhaps what you see is an open field, the place where your structure will eventually be built.) Just notice the state of completion of your vision right now. Notice how perfectly the structure fits into the surrounding landscape. It's as if it were always meant to be there.

Now notice someone standing at the doorway of your structure. It is someone you know, love, and trust—someone who may have been a mentor or teacher for you. They are beckoning you down into the valley. Go to them and greet them. As you stand together in the entryway, look deeply into their eyes. Feel the love and respect they have for you. Then let yourself be taken inside the structure to see it as it is, or as it will be. Let them show you each room, the hallways and all the nooks and crannies. Notice what the walls are made of. Notice the colors. Does this structure have a fragrance or a feeling? Notice if there is any furniture or artwork. Are there any other people in your structure? Can you hear anything? Take a moment to explore your structure, your vision in all its aspects.

Suddenly you notice a long table with a group of architects and engineers clustered around it, looking at the plans for your vision. Join them and let the head architect go over the plans with you. Put your hands on the paper and feel the plans as the architect talks, then ask, "Tell me, what is one thing that I can do right now to make this plan happen?" Listen to the suggestion. It may come as actual words or it may be an image or an intuition about something.

Now turn to the friend who brought you into the structure and notice that they are offering you a wrapped gift box. Take the box, knowing that whatever you find inside is something that represents your vision in the outside world. Open the box and look at the object inside. Every time you see this object, it will act as a symbol to remind you of your vision and let you know you are on the right track. Ask your friend if there is a key word you can use to remind yourself of your vision. Listen and repeat the word they give you.

If you don't see anything inside the box or hear, feel or sense a word, don't worry. You can do this visualization exercise again later. Eventually you'll get an object and a word. It may not be something you can literally see or hear as much as something you sense. Be prepared: your inner critic may try to tell you that you are making all this up. The truth is, you *are* making this up! That's what your imagination does to help you expand beyond the limits of your known self, to create something new.

When you are ready, thank your friend who escorted you, and everyone at the table for their help in making your vision a reality. Go back to the elevator, step inside and visualize the numbers slowly lighting, one a time: 5, 4, 3, 2, 1. When you step out of the elevator, you are back where you began. Before ending this visualization, write down your experience. Remember, every little detail is significant, so be sure to capture them all on paper. By doing this visualization you are creating an inner matrix, a safe haven for you to visit whenever you want to assess what is happening with the vision you have created. Use this visualization any time you want to get information about where you are in your process, or to clarify your next step.

WORKING WITH YOUR SYMBOL

The symbol you received in the visualization exercise is a tool you can use in your daily life to stay connected with your vision. When you are close to something that may lead to your next step, your symbol may appear like a road sign to let you know you are on track.

Phil had been looking for his next career move. He had worked for a software company for many years and had finally left the firm. He needed a new job, but he wanted it to be a good fit, so he went to multiple interviews, searching for the right position. After a couple of months of interviews, he decided that he was working too hard. He thought, "Maybe if I do some inner work I can accelerate my progress." He did the visualization exercise, and the symbol that he received was a BMW, specifically a black BMW 3-Series.

Later that week, he was driving to yet another interview when he noticed that the car in front of him was a black BMW 3-Series. Phil's brain immediately went on high alert. He knew that something was about to happen related to his vision. He also noted with surprise that when he reached his exit, the BMW was also exiting. As he followed the directions to the interview, the BMW stayed directly in front him, and it even turned into the parking lot at his destination. Phil later told me, "It couldn't have been more clear than that! I went into the interview and everything about this job felt right. When they offered it to me, I didn't hesitate. It was a perfect fit."

The symbol has only as much power as you instill in it, so play with this process and see if it works for you too. Now go back to your map and add a drawing of the symbol you saw, or sensed, on the right side. This will remind you when you are on track.

THE PLUS FACTOR

Visualization and working with your imagination, as you did in asking for a symbol and a word, is a way to access your intuition. Intuition is subtle but powerful. New studies describe a "gut" reaction as another sense, along with seeing, smelling, touching, hearing and tasting. That's your intuition, trying to communicate with you. Once you begin to pay attention to that feeling, you will see how often it is working to help you identify the best action to take next.

Here is one of my favorite stories about using your intuition to guide you. My friend Anne wanted a more challenging job and was open to the idea of something different. When she saw an ad for a job at a local board game development company, she decided that it looked like fun, and definitely was different. While she was daydreaming about the job, she got a wacky idea: what if instead of the traditional electronic résumé she was to draw a picture of her résumé? Together we designed her résumé to resemble a very colorful and fun game board—after all, this was a board game company.

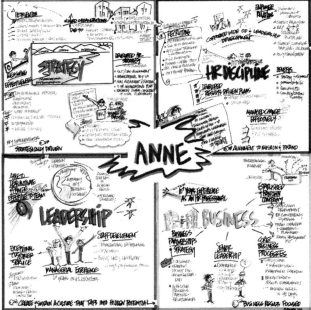

After we created the "picture résumé," we made two copies, and put each of them into a clear plastic tube with the visual facing out so the first thing one saw was a colorful picture. Then we filled the tubes with lots of really cool toys including a set of walkie-talkies. Anne's idea was to put one walkie-talkie in the tube for the CEO and one in the tube for the hiring manager, because as she explained, "They have to be communicating well in order to get the right fit for their positions."

Her unusual resume got their attention! The very next day Anne received a call from the hiring manager. By listening to and following through on her creativity and intuition, she distinguished herself from the other applicants. Let Anne's story inspire you to take your creativity and intuition seriously. The more you do, the stronger they'll become—and so will your confidence and courage.

RISK = GAIN

"If you aren't ahead of the curve of change you risk being irrelevant."
— Rene Godefroy, *Kick Your Excuses Goodbye*

Taking risks is one of the ways to be the initiator of, not the reactor, to the state of your life. Perhaps this involves something as simple as switching child care duties so your spouse gets the kids ready in the morning and you put them to bed at night instead of the other way around. Or the risk could occur in a more public setting: you realize that you want to be the person to run your volunteer board's next strategic planning session. Challenge yourself to do something outside the norm to stay fluid, excited and proactive in all areas of your life. Neuroscientists tell us we are what we think we are. It's been my experience that it's impossible to feel like a victim when I am actively creating my life and my world.

But how can you maintain your creativity when the stress of life starts to creep in? Risk-taking and staying focused on achieving your goals requires that you also give equal time to rest and relaxation. Your planning process should also include making time and space to refill your energy reservoir. Researchers have found that when you are overworked or scared, the amygdala—a very primal part of your brain—tells the adrenal glands to send the hormone cortisol into your blood stream.[1]

When the amygdala is highly stimulated, it can bypass our rational mind making us think everything is threatening. Dr. Neil Neimark says, "We may overreact to the slightest comment. Our fear is exaggerated. Our thinking is distorted. We see everything through the filter of possible danger. We narrow our focus to those things that can harm us. Fear becomes the lens through which we see the world."[2]

Elevated cortisol levels cause marked changes in the way your body functions and have a profound effect on your mood and state of mind. This can result in feelings of panic and self-doubt. All of which causes you to think things like, "Well I can't possibly apply for that job, because they'll ask what kind of experience I have. And all I've done is raise kids for the past twelve years." Poof! Your vision goes up in smoke and you stay stuck in your Current Reality. When you have taken the time to calm yourself down, you will feel more competent at taking risks.

Even the simple act of making a "to-do" list, and noting why the items scare you, will help calm down your amygdala. High school students who wrote down their fears in advance of their ACT test actually showed a 15 percent increase in their test-taking success.[3] Your brain looks at your list, sorts for things you know how to do and red flags the ones that are more difficult. The difficult and scary ones will stretch you and help you reach those goals. By calming yourself down and taking things one step at a time, you will reinforce your confidence that you can do this! Taking risks may be scary but they are essential to make a dream come true.

If you don't take risks, you are stuck in a box. The box can constrain any part of your life to keep you from growing and changing. For example, what if your response to the Desired New Reality side of your map is, "These outcomes really aren't possible!" Peter McWilliams, author of *You Can't Afford A Negative Thought* reminds us, "Our thoughts become reality; where we put our attention is where we tend to go." Challenge yourself to step out of your comfort zone, focus on what you want, revisit your old attitudes to see if they are still working for you. You can keep pace with the changes you are making both inside and out. Feel the fear and do it anyway.

TAKE TIME FOR YOURSELF

Molly is a successful theatre director with three sons. As her youngest sons were about to finish high school and leave home for college, she felt very excited about embarking on a new stage of her life as an "empty nester"—able to do whatever she liked with her free time. A sudden death in her extended family orphaned two young children. Because Molly is a sweet, wonderful, generous and practical soul, she adopted the two children. Six months later, she realized that the dramatic change in her life circumstances had generated considerable stress. Her dreams about a life that was not centered on parenting were going to be postponed for many years.

Smart woman that she is, she did two things. First, she made arrangements for her family to begin to see a therapist; and second, she decided to take time every day to go for a walk with her dog, by herself. Everyone in the family was notified that her time walking the dog was her quiet time to think and reflect. By working with the therapist, everyone had a place to go to talk about the emotions generated by the new family configuration. And by carving out time for herself away from the demands of family life, Molly got the time she desperately needed.

Almost everyone I know complains about not having enough time in the day to get everything done. When you are really living your life, engaged in what you feel passionate about, you can find yourself so excited and motivated that you push yourself to do more. That Desired New Reality looks pretty good, and it seems reasonable to think that if you stay up later, get up earlier and work longer, your new life will manifest faster.

However, as your intentions result in new opportunities and challenges, or when unexpected developments occur, as in the case of Molly and her brand-new family, it is critical that you take steps to ride out the changes with balance and grace. If living a balanced life was not included among the goals for your Desired New Reality, consider adding this now and decide which Bold Steps and Action Steps you will include to that.

While you are working toward your goals and visions, take time daily to step outside the business of everyday life to reflect and just be quiet. Whether you are a stay-at-home mom or President of the United States, everyone needs down time alone. How will you designate your own "dog walking time?" If you make this a priority, your friends and family will adjust. You simply need to work it out inside yourself first. If you let your life run away from you, you can easily find yourself feeling victimized. Just a few days ago, you may have offered to help someone out, but now suddenly *you resent that they expect you to do what you offered.* If you take care of yourself, making time to rest and reflect, you make it possible to feel, and do, your best. Incorporate this time into your larger plan and you will find it easier to keep your balance, and your focus.

COMPARE YOURSELF ONLY TO YOU

We live in a culture that glorifies competiveness. And we have a tendency to compare ourselves to others as a way of gauging our own expectations of ourselves. Comparing yourself to people you admire can be a source of inspiration, but it can also make you feel that you're better or worse than everyone else. As Eckhart Tolle writes, "Comparison is in service to the ego."[4] A drama therapist colleague of mine, Christopher, goes even further: "Comparison is violence."

Each of us changes at our own pace, no matter how rapidly or slowly someone else might want us to change. How quickly we adapt to change is also influenced by our own perception of how well we have adapted in the past. In his book, *The Biology of Belief*, Bruce Lipton reinforces the idea that our expectations and beliefs determine the outcome of what and how we experience our world. Expectations can be constrained by limited thinking. Use all your new tools to set positive, expansive expectations and manage changes as they occur, even when that includes steering your ship around other people's perceptions to stay on your own course.

"For, he that expects nothing shall not be disappointed, but he that expects much—if he lives and uses that in hand day by day—shall be full to running over."

—*Edgar Cayce*

REPLACE THE THINGS THAT NO LONGER ALIGN

When you create your map, you will clearly see that many of the things you included in your Current Reality have hindered your ability to create the life you want. As you work with your map, you may also find that there are goals or desires under the Desired New Reality that are no longer relevant, or need to be modified to reflect the changes you are going through as you work your Bold Steps and Action Steps. For example, you may have included "Get a new car" as a goal. Along the way, you may decide that your commitment to environmental sustainability has influenced the kind of car you visualize for yourself and now your goal is "Get a new hybrid car."

The Desired New Reality is definitely the place to identify your dreams. Yet as you yourself transform through the process of taking your intuition and creativity seriously, your dreams may likewise change. In fact, the entire process is one of constant refinement as you find that some things you initially wanted lose their importance.

A single friend of mine had two goals: adopt a child and attract a partner for a committed relationship. When she met her partner and found that many of her emotional needs were being met in that relationship, she realized that the desire to adopt a child had diminished. As your life evolves and changes, you do too. Take time to revaluate and, if necessary, redefine your dreams. Perhaps you unconsciously included them due to old family beliefs or because you felt you should.

I like to have on hand plenty of what I call "Oops Tape": self-stick labels that I place over any area of my map I want to change to reflect more accurately what is going on for me right now.

Exercise: Map "Performance Evaluation"

Schedule a session with yourself, about three months after you create your map, to review it from an overarching perspective. Scan the images and words you have written as if you were reviewing your job performance at work. Notice if everything you included as goals are still important and, if necessary, fine-tune your words or images. This check-in process also provides the opportunity to celebrate your accomplishments and brainstorm new ways to approach what's left to do. The map is an iterative process. When it reflects what is real for you right now, you keep it fresh and alive as you enhance your belief in and dedication to your dreams.

HURRY UP AND BE PATIENT

In this constant state of change, it's difficult to know the right dance steps to keep moving to the beat. Be patient. We live in a world of instantaneous results: if you are hungry, there's fast food so you can eat NOW. The Internet answers any question you can think of with just a few keystrokes. If you live in the U.S., you can purchase items online, from groceries to furniture, even if you don't have the cash to pay for it. In such a world it is difficult to feel patient when what you want to change isn't happening *right now*.

As you wait for things to fall into place, what do you do about the inevitable anxiety? Continue to do all the little things you know will help move you toward your goals. A friend who hopes to support himself as a working artist has been struggling to show a profit from sales of his work. To support his art and pay the bills he has had to take on lots of odd jobs, from lawn care to mural painting. The odds seem stacked against him: very few people are able to make a living as an artist in the U.S. As the years go by, and the big money and recognition still elude him, he is undeterred. He believes, without a shadow of a doubt, the day will come when his art and his business will take off. He told me his secret for staying on track and motivated. It's quite simple: every day he asks Life, "Now what? What do you want me to do today?" Then he takes action on every opportunity or intuitive nudge that comes his way, and continues to move towards his goal. His determination and patience are remarkable.

What this all boils down to is: you must determine what you want to change, do everything you can to make that change happen, and then be patient while the universe restructures things so you can live your dream fulfilled.

When I began to take part in bike races, my first goal was to place in the top ten in a race. All my training went toward that goal. When I reached it, I set my sights on placing in the top five. In time, I achieved that goal and began to consider a new goal, winning first place. I trained harder and rode longer, and sometimes I did well and other times not so well. As the season ended that year, placing first still eluded me.

Then I noticed that most of the riders who came in ahead of me were half my age, while I almost always finished ahead of the riders who were my age and at my level. Was my ability to reach my goal being affected by the context of where I chose to compete? When I began to consider this, I discovered that the best context for me as a middle-aged bike racer was in the Senior Olympics. It never occurred to me that once I turned 50, I was considered a senior! In the Senior Olympics bike races, competing against women in my own category, my abilities as a racer were more evenly matched and I achieved my goal of claiming that first place podium spot.

While it is important to set goals and work toward them, what I learned from bike racing is it is also important to look for what you might be missing. If your plan is thorough and things still aren't happening as you hoped, step back, relax your focus and see if there is something you haven't taken into consideration that may be affecting your chances of success.

Then, like my artist friend, ask the universe, "What next? What do you want me to do today?" If you have been sharing your process with other people, ask them what they think you might be missing. You will often get some good ideas. No matter how long it seems to take, you will continue to feel confident if you stay focused on where you are going.

Make a list, review your map, call a friend, or take a walk. Be patient.

BE GRATEFUL

While determination, patience, faith and trust all play big roles in the process, gratitude keeps them all in harmony, and keeps the changes coming. No matter how rotten things may appear, there is always something tangible to be grateful for: your health, the support of your friends and family, the smile of a stranger when you feel discouraged, the beauty of the tree outside your window.

At a recent workshop, the facilitator gave each of us a "gratitude journal" and suggested we write down three things we were grateful for each night before we went to sleep. She also suggested that each night we tell our partner three things about them that we are grateful for. When you cultivate a sense of gratitude, it smoothes and oils the tracks so your rickety old cart of visions, dreams and goals can travel smoothly towards the future.

Another way to express gratitude is to think about people in your circle of friends and family, work world or neighborhood and send thanks and love to them. Reflect on your good fortune for having them in your life and consciously wish them well. While you are at it, why not send your gratitude for all the people who live in your state, your nation, and throughout the world in every nation? Love everyone and everything and thank them as fully as you can. Finally, simply send gratitude radiating out of yourself into the universe.

You can accelerate your progress by looking for ways to perform one secret act of kindness for someone you don't know. This can be as simple as letting a harried mother with a small child move ahead of you in line at the post office. Take a moment when you notice someone who is having a difficult time and send love to him or her. Watch how any of these simple acts of kindness come back to you and fill your heart with gratitude.

BECOME YOUR OWN BIGGEST FAN

When you embark on a new venture, in addition to all the planning and visualizing, you also need supporters, or at least one die-hard fan who will cheer you on as you celebrate your successes and ride out your failures. When I first started out as a performance artist, writing and producing my own shows, I was just out of college and living on a shoestring. I had fabulous ideas for the shows I planned to write and perform, but almost no budget for sets or costumes. When I was mounting my first show, I turned to my mother for help in sewing my first costumes. She was an amazing seamstress who had created one-of-a-kind costumes that she and my father wore to costume parties.

My mother arrived in Seattle ready to help, and I set her up in a friend's apartment with a borrowed sewing machine. Together we created all my costumes for my first big show, and when she was finished sewing, she helped paint the sets. At the last minute, she even offered to be my dresser during the performance. She provided me with unwavering confidence in my vision—not only of my performance in that show, but also my identity as a successful artist. We shared the thrill of the theatre and had a great time doing it.

Whenever I was writing a new show, she would wistfully say, "Oh, if you would just do that Lucky Dog show again, now *that* was a great show." Years later, long after I had stopped performing, she would make the same comment. It became a running gag with my friends and siblings. To this day, when I start complaining about something, they will look me in the eye and say, "Oh, if only you'd do that Lucky Dog Show again." I always laugh; it reminds me of the incredible support she provided me. She was my biggest fan.

Over the years, my mother saved every playbill, press clipping, review, poster or picture from each of my shows. She carefully framed and hung them all on the walls of my childhood bedroom. My brother and sister laughingly referred to my old room as "the shrine."

For me, it was an amazing feeling to walk into that room and look around. I felt embarrassed, but also filled with deep sense of pride. Her belief in me was a gift that gave me a constant source of motivation. No matter how many doubts I had about my career and abilities, my mother's belief in me and my vision was a constant reminder that I could succeed as an actor.

After my mother transitioned out of this life, it left a big hole in my fan base. One day, I felt so overwhelmed and so missed her support, I broke down and had a really long cry. Then it occurred to me: the best way I could honor my mother was to become my own biggest fan. I liked the idea. I could give myself the same encouragement and faith I had relied on for so many years. But how would I do this? Would I ever be able to silence my inner critic? Could I trust all of my wacky ideas and give myself positive feedback? Deciding to be my own biggest fan was the first step in my own journey of self-acceptance. I realized then that an important ingredient in success—yours or mine—is to accept the fact that you need a fan. That fan may be someone close to you who believes in you. But because your dream is only as powerful you believe it can be, be sure that one of your biggest fans is you.

HOW TO WORK WITH THE SCARED OR CRITICAL PART OF YOUR BRAIN

Your mind likes routines. When you try to change the way you do things, be prepared for some resistance. Imagine that you are a fast-food person who has decided to make a sweeping change in your diet. From now on you are going to buy only whole foods and cook everything yourself! Full of determination, you set out for the grocery store. Once you arrive in the produce section and survey all of the vegetables, that inner voice begins to remind you: all this cooking is going to take a lot of time, and stocking your kitchen is going to be expensive. You begin to feel anxious.

Then you notice a sign touting a fantastic discount on your favorite frozen pizza. That voice in your mind says, "Yeah!" It would be so much less stressful to just toss a few pizzas in your cart and get back to more important things. And before you know it, you are whistling as you cross the parking lot to your car without a single vegetable in your shopping bag. Your mind just won this round. The challenge of doing something new or different has been sidelined, for now.

How many times has a friend announced their plan to do something radically different in their life, and a few weeks later you run into them and ask about the new program. What new program? Doing the familiar, even if it keeps them miserable, is easier than grappling with change.

The part of your brain that prefers the familiar is also responsible for torpedoing great ideas before they become your Bold Steps or Desired New Reality. The limbic system of your brain determines how you react to sensual stimulation. In many cases it is critical for survival, allowing you to react with lighting speed when someone pulls out in front of your car. It is also to blame when you spontaneously yell at someone who took your parking place. This sets off the merry-go-round of the anger response, which, along with diminished ability to learn new things, has been linked to anxiety attacks or depression.

As overwhelming as this may sound, the great thing about how your brain works is this: it is only responding to the cues you provide. You can actually trick it into responding differently!

For example, when you created your map, you came up with your big Bold Steps—the things you decided to do to manifest your New Desired Reality. At the time it may have felt thrilling to think about taking the leap, to do things differently, to make big changes. Now, a week or a month later, you look at those Bold Steps and they feel completely daunting. You may wonder how in the world you are going to do them. Doubt begins to seep in, followed by fear, and before long your cortisol levels begin to rise, and, well, you know where this is all headed …

Exercise: Switching Off Your Amygdala

Here's a simple way to stop this cascade of events. First, notice and label what you are feeling. This is called "symbolic labeling."[5] This activates a part of your brain that "puts the brakes" on escalating reactions.

"I'M SORRY TRISH, YOU DIDN'T GET THE JOB"

Next, identify even one small, easy step you can take to move closer to your goals. Setting up small, manageable tasks that you can easily complete will calm your amygdala and reduce the tendency to spiral into negativity.

Let's say one of your big Bold Steps is to "Quit My Job." A simple, manageable task might be to make a list of what you liked about the jobs you have had in the past. Then make sure you have captured all those qualities in your New Desired Reality. You could also make a list of the people you know who have found satisfaction by quitting their jobs, and call them to talk about it.

The act of doing something different in a familiar situation begins to rewire your brain for healthier responses in similar situations. Simply put, you can learn to bypass your amygdala's automatic default operations, in much the same way you choose to tap different buttons on a computer to enter a new screen.

When you find yourself in a negative, fear-based place, here are five things you can do to switch your brain into a more positive place:

1. Do something physical that makes you sweat. Any form of activity in which you work up a sweat for five minutes will help prevent buildup of stress hormones

2. Put on some music and dance around

3. Pet your dog or cat

4. Call one of your upbeat friends

5. Find a funny video on YouTube and laugh out loud

All of these are simple relaxation techniques to help get that pesky amygdala out of the way and make room for more creative ideas. The more skilled you become at noting when you are stressing out from fear or self-criticism, naming it and reprogramming your response to shift yourself back into a positive place, the easier it will be for you to get back to taking action on your New Desired Reality plan.

YOUR CHANGE AND ITS IMPACT ON EVERYONE ELSE: TUNING IN

According to Quantum Physics, we are all composed of vibrating matter, and all life is simply little molecules spinning and swirling around in a whirl of energy.

When you change the way you think and act, and begin to use visual imagery to generate the things you want in life, your energetic pattern changes. By changing your habits, you also begin to resonate to a new and different frequency.

You could say you are "tuning" yourself to a new song. In doing so, you *surrender* to small shifts in yourself and those around you. What I mean by surrender is, you acknowledge that you are available for divine intervention, in whatever form it materializes, to help you along. These shifts are simply change energy. What can that change energy do? In a family, it may feel scary. You're no longer the partner or spouse or sibling they're used to. The more information you can provide everyone around you about the changes you are initiating, and why, the more likely they will be able to adapt. But you must give them something to tune into.

If, until now, you have a history of talking about change but not really making it, be prepared for some surprised reactions when you actually follow through on your plan. Keep in mind that the way people react to your efforts is directly related to their own comfort level with change. Those who are flexible and able to adapt to their own changes will be in a better place to offer suggestions or help. If making change isn't easy for them, they may respond by creating obstacles for you or giving you a big dose of their own fears.

Change creates holes in the fabric of daily life. It forces you to look deeply at yourself and others, and sometimes you may not like what you see. Get in touch with your deepest, most authentic self— the one that approaches life with a playful, childlike curiosity. It will help you be fully present to what is happening within and around you.

SHARING YOUR VISION

After an individual session with a Snapshot of the Big Picture map, most of the people I work with are excited and passionate about sharing their new vision with *everyone*. Many of them carry their maps around, showing anyone who will listen—at home, with friends and at work.

Not a good idea. Not everyone is as overjoyed as you are about your Desired New Reality. For this reason, I encourage you to be protective of your new vision. Sharing it with someone who reacts with doubt or fear may challenge your own confidence. One way to decide who might be supportive is to reflect on their past responses to your changes and ideas. To keep your own enthusiasm high, list the people you feel you can count on to be supportive of your vision, and separately list those who may not. This is particularly true if you have people in your life who have been critical or even scared of changes in the past. You may discover that some people feel it is their duty to protect you from disappointment or failure.

I encourage you to only share the map and your vision with people who will positively support you in achieving it. While you have a responsibility to be honest and open, timing is everything. When your dream is new, it is a delicate seed of an idea, and you must protect it. This is one way to honor yourself and your process. Some of us find it easy to honor others but have difficulty doing it with ourselves. Now is the time to surround yourself with the kind of positivity that will protect and propel your vision into the future.

UNDERSTANDING THOSE DIVERSE REACTIONS

One of the most painful parts of mapping your future is encountering people you love and trust who seem intent on sabotaging your progress. It happens all the time. Suddenly all sorts of reasons come up for waiting until later or changing your priorities. Because people you respect are presenting these very legitimate detours, it is hard to say no and keep to your plan. These well-meaning people may include your parents, partners or spouse, best friends, colleagues and most precious confidantes, all of whom feel it's their right to challenge your thinking.

When you share your Desired New Reality, be prepared for anything. The listener may appear distracted or even disinterested. They might interrupt or dismiss you. And they may totally freak out! Your inner confidence may waver when you pour your heart out and the response implies they don't think your plan is sound. Expect them to look you in the eye and solemnly say, "I've known you for a long time and I think you need to …"

Once you get over any disappointment and beat back your self-doubt, go back to your core. Your core is that part of yourself that knows the next step for you, despite the whirl of the things and people around you. One way to reconnect to your core is to call up the symbol you saw or repeat the word you were given in the Visualization exercise, that brings a sense of peace and alignment. Bring your focus to that which you desire in the future. The images will reboot that initial state of euphoria you felt when you first created your map.[6]

You may need to reassess, especially if the negative response comes from someone close to you. Ask yourself, "What is the right thing for me to do with this reaction? Is there anything about what they've said that I need to take into consideration? Will acting on their suggestions or concerns help me move towards my desired goals? Or is this response being generated by fear of change?"

While you don't want to be derailed from carrying out your plan, some modifications may be called for. When your income is the sole support for others, you have a responsibility to work it out with everyone concerned, to create a realistic plan to make the changes you want. And there is no law that says you can't make changes to your plan when it's not working for you anymore.

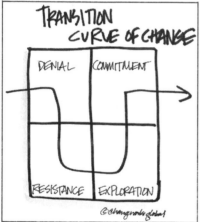

The important thing is to ask them directly for the support you need and lay out your expectations of what this may mean for them. Then be flexible, curious and open while you listen to their reaction. Remember to stay the course that's right for you.

There are many theories about how each of us moves through the phases of major change. When I was working as a consultant with the team at Changeworks Global, the firm's founders, Cynthia Scott and Dennis Jaffe, had coined a term: **The Transition Curve**[7] (T-Curve).

As the illustration shows the first phase is *Denial*. We don't want to deal with the reality of change, so we stick our head in the sand and wish it would go away. This is followed by *Resistance*: we get mad, complain, and use any trick we can think of to resist changing. Then we move into *Exploration* and start to take an honest look at all of our options. Finally we embrace *Commitment*. We step fully into the experience of transition and become committed to following through with the changes that are occurring.

In the mapping process, Denial might show up by believing that all the Bold Steps and Actions are going to be a breeze and will happen instantaneously: that form of denial could also be called uninformed optimism. Resistance is generated by the parts of us that get mired in self-doubt and self-critical thinking. Exploration is what the Desired New

Reality is all about. Commitment is walking over the Bold Step bridges that bring us to our Desired New Reality. The T-Curve is a powerful tool to help you understand the impact of change and how it is affecting you and those around you.

Each of us moves through those phases at our own pace. It may be that you are enjoying the euphoric dance of exploration or the firm zeal of commitment, while those around you are still surprised that something needed to change at all. Keep the T-Curve in mind when first presenting your need to make changes. Take a step back, and remember they may be starting off in the denial phase, so your job is to gently walk them through your whole process.

At any rate, it's better to start dropping hints early when you are considering a change that involves other people and their welfare. As a teenager, I saw this play out when my father faced either quitting his long-time job or being shuffled into a dead-end position. Since he was a company man who had only worked for two firms in his entire career, he was devastated. My father was a smart and proud man and was angry and at a loss about what do to next. My mother, fortunately, was skilled at adapting to changes. Over dinners in the weeks that followed, she exuded optimism and belief in his ability to adapt. She encouraged him to see this as a chance to do something new and even better.

My father eventually parlayed his many years of engineering experience as a concrete specialist to create a lucrative and successful consulting career with companies around the world. Twenty-five years later he was given a lifetime achievement award for his contributions to the field of concrete engineering!

If you are facing a major change and like my father, feeling angry and at a loss, garnering the support of one or two other people can bolster your courage to move forward. Invite help by being honest and open about your doubts and fears. You may even be surprised who steps up with support.

SELECTIVE SHARING

When you embark on major change—perhaps with little more than a shoestring of a budget and a map of a dream—you are also the most vulnerable to the opinions of others.

I previously cautioned you about sharing your Snapshot map and vision, and want to reiterate that it takes selective sharing to find positive, reassuring support for your journey. Here is how I learned discretion.

When I wanted to shift my career from being a therapist to working with businesses, I made the mistake of mentioning it to my neighbor—who was also my landlord. She was a person who had been doing the same job of teaching for her entire career. She took one look at my map and went into a tailspin. "How do you know that you'll be good at consulting? Do you have enough savings to tide you over?" And so forth. Despite having successfully changed careers before, I suddenly found myself doubting my abilities and I stalled out for about three months. Gradually, I realized her reaction stemmed from her own fear that I would be unable to pay rent. It was not an accurate assessment of my capacity for successful change. By understanding that and spending time with people who were excited and positive about making changes, I got back on track.

Change brings out the best and worst in us all. Stay true to yourself and avoid anyone who may try to dump a truckload of fear or negativity on your brilliant plan.

HOW TO MITIGATE NEGATIVITY

If you are faced with negativity, try these strategies:

1. Consider the source. Does this person feel trapped in some aspect of their life, unhappy with their job, home, relationships, family? Keep your distance from what they are saying to you. Remember, their negative reaction is a reflection of them, not you. It tells you what kind of person they are and what issues they may be dealing with. It's not a reflection of you or your plan.

2. Remain detached. Most people want you to engage in a dialogue with them. One of my long-time friends absolutely loves to poke holes in anything. She is not a negative person; she just wants to understand things better. Her style can feel like an attack. As a result, whenever I have an idea I want to protect, I have found it best not to engage in debate about its validity, but rather to let her wind down her questioning before I clarify my point of view. Pretend you are sitting across from yourself and watching your own reactions as someone responds to or critiques your ideas. Note what surfaces without getting caught up in the

emotions. When your emotions are running the show, you tend to be reactive rather than proactive. Stay calm.

3. Find the truth in the comment. If you have a knee-jerk, "No that's not it!" reaction, you can be sure there is a nugget of truth there. One response is to simply take note of it, rather than defending your position. You don't have to unravel it right then, even if they want you to. Ask them to say more about what they are thinking or feeling; clarify their comments. See if you can find a clue about what triggered your response. Later, you can go back and examine the comment to determine the truth within it. Imagine that, like an image or symbol you received in a dream, their comment contains a gift.

4. Remain positive. Studies show that you can influence, and be influenced, by those around you. However, if your energy remains steadfastly positive, it will override any negativity that comes your way.

In the early '90s I worked as an artist-in-residence in the San Bruno County Jail. After my first day working there, I became very sick as soon as I got home. I'm normally a very healthy person, so I was shocked at the severity of my illness. As I suffered through that long night of fever, I realized that the negativity of consciousness inside the jail was immense. I wasn't prepared for the intensity of that energy; it hit me like a ton of bricks. I recovered the next day, but from then on, whenever I arrived at the jail, I would encase myself in a thick bubble of protection as I waited to pass through security. I visualized a membrane of protection that allowed my energy to flow out so I could work effectively, but would block any negative influences coming my way. The jail's negativity never influenced me again. Raise your own positive energy so you are filtering out anything that might deplete you.

WORKING THROUGH YOUR RESENTMENT TO CHANGE

Nobody likes being forced to change. Before you begin to shift yourself into taking your next step, you will have to deal with your reactions. Here is a simple technique that will help you sort out and understand them.

Exercise: Reactions and Drivers

At the top of a piece of paper, write an issue that prompted strong feelings of resentment in you. It may even be when you lost your job, or your relationship ended, or your house was in foreclosure. Or it may be your reaction to one of your Bold Steps. Draw a line down the center of the page. On one side write the word REACTIONS. On the other side write DRIVERS.

Now write and draw your reactions to what happened to you. Ask yourself, "What am I experiencing? What am I feeling, thinking, and seeing around me?" In the other column, write and draw the drivers behind what you are feeling. "What is driving it? Am I mad? Why? Didn't they tell me what was going to happen? Did my relationship end abruptly? Am I sad? Why?" Draw a picture of it. Write a quote that expresses the essence of how you are feeling: "I thought we were making progress in our relationship and now I'm really disappointed!"

After a few minutes, look at what you have written and drawn. The goal is neither to interpret nor clarify, but simply to make sure you have captured what you are thinking and feeling. Then, find someone to talk to about what happened. Just saying it out loud gives voice to everything you have secretly been thinking and feeling in isolation. If you can't find someone to tell your story to, then write about it. Write about what you see on your page.

The hardest place to be is on your own in the middle of a change. It isn't unusual to feel victimized and distressed. By bringing your feelings into the light of day, you help yourself process and gain distance from your emotions.

Acording to David Rock[8], another way to help yourself work through your reactions, once you have acknowledged what you are feeling, is to reframe or reappraise what has happened. There are four types of reappraisal:

- *Re-interpretation*—You decide that what you once thought of as a threat is no longer threatening. For example, consultants are reviewing the structure of how things get done where you work. At first you think you might lose your job, and

you are filled with panic. You read the memo again and realize the processes they are examining are not within your department. Your anxiety goes down.

- *Normalizing*—You look over your Action Steps list and realize the changes you are facing make you feel scared and anxious. You remind yourself, this is a typical reaction for what you are experiencing.

- *Re-ordering*—You liked meeting new people at the job you had, and now you are being moved into a position where you will have a better title, but less interaction with others. Your brain has placed "being with others" at the top of the list of things that bring you satisfaction. You take a moment to list the advantages of your new level: now you actually have the ability to improve how things are done. This helps your brain re-order your priorities and helps calm you down.

- *Re-positioning*—You take the position of someone else to expand your view of what is happening. Look through their eyes. "How would my partner view this change?" "How is my boss viewing this change?" This may be the hardest reappraising technique.

Any of these suggestions will help you create order during the chaos and set you up for more success moving forward. You can't hide your feelings or reactions; you have to clear the stuff you are holding inside. That negative debris will interfere with your ability to adapt and find creative solutions. It must shift to make room for something new. Writing and drawing about it, or using any of the reappraisal techniques, gives you distance from your experience. This helps you shift from Denial and Resistance into Exploration—where your natural curiosity about the future gets you creative and excited about how to ride out the changes.

GETTING THROUGH FEAR TO EXPOSE THE TRUTH

Fear is one of the main reasons people don't change. Just the thought of switching jobs, ending a relationship, moving to a new place or doing things differently can keep us rooted in the past and reliving old patterns even if they no longer feel good.

With change comes an inevitable and sometimes chaotic adjustment period, as we try to understand where the path is leading us. As I was completing my psychology degree, I knew that being a therapist wasn't exactly my dream career. But I'd invested so much time and money getting through school that even though I was feeling bored and listless, I was determined to make things work. I didn't realize it then, but the fact that I had to force myself to continue to my drama therapy practice was the first clue that this line of work wasn't for me.

Because I wasn't willing to acknowledge my discomfort, the universe stepped in to make it perfectly clear. In the span of one month, the angry husband of one of my patients stalked me, a fistfight broke out during a family therapy session, and I received a court subpoena for my practice notes. Still reeling from all of this, the last nail in the coffin was when my supervisor, who was also a close friend, confessed that she was sleeping with a patient. I had no choice but to report her breach of ethics to the head of the department, and she lost her job. Not long after this, I left the therapy field, with no idea what I would do next.

I was immediately offered an opportunity to do pro bono teambuilding and change management sessions for a corporate consulting firm. I quickly realized how I would use my drama therapy training to create a new career. I found I was really good at facilitating large groups of employees who were angry about layoffs or restructuring in their work-place. I drew on my training to calm and focus groups that were being faced with immense changes. I found drama everywhere in these settings, to put it mildly! Helping people role-play new behaviors, or coming up with creative interactive experiences for corporate groups was a natural next step for me. Looking back, I could never have predicted that my dissatisfaction with conventional therapy work would lead me to where I am today—fully engaged in a unique career where I apply all my skills every day.

In a thin little handbook entitled *Guiding Yourself Into a Spiritual Reality*, authors Peggy Dylan and Tolly Burkan, founders of the modern fire walking movement, talk about fear as an integral part of the unknown that comes wedded  to adventurous territory. Fear, they write, is False Evidence Appearing Real, simply a construct of the mind.

They take the experience of successful fire walking and break it into small steps to show how you can overcome fear and live your life more fully. At the time I read this, it felt like my fingers were on one cliff edge and my toes on another, and I was trying to find the courage to let go and leap. This book gave me some much-needed distance and perspective. I began to recognize that many of my fears were assumptions about what I was capable of or what I would find. I learned that all change requires some element of risk, but when you start to break it down, those fearful assumptions come from that part of your brain that wants to keep you protected and safe. What the brain doesn't have stored in its long-term memory, it creates a story about. Often that story is not based in reality, but is a cobbling together of assumptions that produce unwarranted anxiety.

Our culture bombards us with fear stories. The nightly news, advertisements, many

religions and the mindset of people around you all reflect the belief that the world is a dangerous place. Fear is only a construct of the mind, but when you give it power, it becomes real.

How can you navigate big changes and unknown outcomes and still get beyond your fears? The prefrontal cortex, the part of your brain engaged in decision-making, actually expands when you adopt a positive frame of mind, opening you to more creativity and flexibility in developing solutions.[9] Fear constrains your ability to do this. And the long-term effects of negativity actually result in a much narrower view of the problem and range of solutions.

A technique I use to deal with fear is to bring myself into a state of mindfulness: being fully present to the experience that is eliciting fear. When fear paralyzes my ability to think clearly, a shift in awareness will free me to see other perspectives. I stop what I am doing, put my feet on the ground, and take a few slow, deep breaths.

Recently, while dining out, I got into a conversation with our young waitress. She had recently had her first baby and was still reeling from the resulting life changes. Caring for that baby at all hours of the day had left her sleep deprived. At times she felt completely overwhelmed and scared. She realized she was totally responsible for this tiny new life, and she feared she was not up to the task. She confided in me that her mother's advice completely transformed her attitude: "Always remember, she is just a baby and crying is the only way she knows how to communicate. You aren't doing anything wrong." After that, whenever the baby cried, she would remind herself it wasn't an emergency. The

young woman had become mindful in the present moment. As a result, she was able to care for and nurture her child in the face of her inexperience.

To manage your own fear, calm down and find the truth about the situation.

Here are some conventionally held beliefs:

• Many new businesses fail

• This may not be the best time to launch a new venture

• It is harder to find a partner as you get older

Yet stories abound of people who have made new businesses work, or succeeded in a down economy or found partners with which to share the final chapters of their life. There are very likely people who have accomplished all three.

Whatever your Bold Steps and Desired New Reality are, you can face fear and move forward. I witnessed a profound example of this while consulting with a big financial institution during the stock market downturn in the late 1990s. The company had been on a hiring spree, adding 1,000 employees to the payroll shortly before the market bubble burst. I was brought in to help the human resources team as they orchestrated a major staff reduction.

They assembled all the employees who were being laid off in one room, and put those who were to stay in another. Then they told all the employees who were losing their jobs to clean out their desks and leave as quickly and quietly as they could. They were not able to say good-bye to anyone and they had no opportunity for closure. Then they told the remaining employees what had happened. The reaction was anger toward the leadership of the company and the way the layoffs had been handled.

At this point that I was brought in to design a listening session between management and the angry employees. The aim was to give them a chance to air their feelings and rebuild the group so they could move forward to revive the company.

When I began, the management team said they wished they could go back in time and change the decisions that got them in this fix. In particular, the company vice president regretted that the increased staff had stretched the company finances too thin once the stock market tanked. However, going back in time was not an option, and the company was a mess.

We held a number of sessions where the employees were able to air their grievances. As a rule, managers dread such meetings and avoid them if at all possible, or pass the buck about who is responsible.

In this case something amazing happened. The vice president responsible for the rapid hiring voluntarily attended every session, where she not only answered questions but owned her decision. Publicly. She told them, "I am responsible for this terrible mistake. I hired people too quickly. I don't expect to be forgiven for what has happened, and I share your sadness at losing many fine colleagues and friends. I want you to be mad at me, not the company."

At each session, I watched her step right into the fire to speak her truth. She certainly must have had trepidation, yet she did it anyway. There was no attempt to downplay what had happened and the impact it had on all concerned. Her leadership and courage will stay with me forever, because I witnessed how the truth transformed and healed everyone. When you stand in your truth and speak from that place in service to your highest good, fear is banished and change is possible.

GUIDING YOURSELF THROUGH THE CHANGE PROCESS: KEEP ALERT FOR THE "OUT OF THE BLUE"

Changes you want to make based on your Snapshot map sometimes show up in a strange package you don't remember ordering. You thought you wanted X and one day Y shows up. When this happens, it is a good time to start investigating: "What is this about? Why did they ask me to do this weird thing at my job?"

When something shows up out of the blue, check your mindset to see if your reaction is linked to an old pattern or belief. Does that new boss (and how he just responded to you in the meeting) look like the old boss from your former company? If so, there's still something going on inside for you to work out.

Are you experiencing something out of the ordinary? Pay closer attention. If I had never followed up on those phone messages and gone to audition for Bill's show, I might never have been on Broadway. When I got the messages, aside from being desperate, I was curious. I had never auditioned for another person's show; this was new for me. I bumbled my way through the dance steps well enough to get cast, though in a limited role.

In each scene, the dancers would all eventually "die" in a hilarious send-up on performance art. Because I was so bad at the dance combinations, the directors decided it was better to kill me off at the beginning of every sequence.

I decided to become the best dead body I could possibly be. In fact, I eventually became the "featured dead body!" They even printed "Dead Body" instead of my name on my show coat. As a result, I got more live exposure than many of the other supporting cast members, simply by lying dead onstage for almost the entire show while Bill Irwin and others danced around me. Just think, Kate Hepburn and Carol Channing watched me lie there dead!

The path that leads to where you are supposed to be may take a circuitous route. You're curious, so you go to a job interview that isn't exactly what you want—only to find that the person conducting the interview makes your heart flip and eventually becomes your spouse. Or you may not be the right person for the job, but the interviewer knows of another position in another firm that would be perfect fit for you. And so it goes.

How many stories have you heard that ended just this way? When you believe that each step you take is happening just for you, your stress level decreases and you enjoy the process more. When people say "change is easy for me," it means they have learned to accept what shows up out of the blue and aren't afraid to work with it. You don't know where the step in front of you will lead, but if you waste time feeling upset because it's not what you expected, you might miss out on what's possible.

Most of the time we neither expect nor know how to accept something that appears out of the blue. It's as if we create the map and then put on a blindfold. Blind faith isn't how you change beliefs. Beliefs and patterns change when you keep your awareness sharp enough to recognize and discern subtle guidance, and then use it to link together the pieces of the puzzle when they appear.

Expand your focus to include both the individual aspects of your map and the whole big picture.

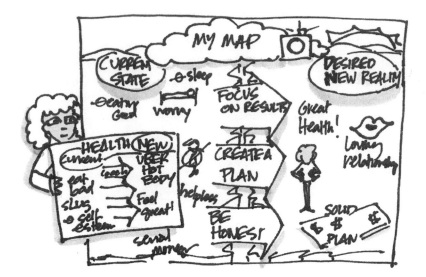

You may find other parts of the map are just as important as the part you're currently working on. There may be an order to manifestation, unique to you. Keep alert to everything that comes your way, because any one of those steps you didn't count on is part of the magic choreography that will dance you into your desired future.

SHAKE HANDS WITH CHANGE

In your own mind, you have become a change expert. Then suddenly your life partner, parent, teacher, or beloved child makes a change. AARRGH! All those great coping mechanisms go sailing out the window. Perhaps you don't feel quite the tolerance for their change as you did for your own. Now you're on the receiving end. This is a just a deeper, more intense change because the people you love are also changing all around you. Do you find yourself thinking you don't want them to change, you like them just the way they are?

The people who bring change upon us unwittingly become catalysts for our own growth, but don't often earn our gratitude. On a talk show, a host interviewed a woman who had been fired from her job. As a result, the woman went on to make a huge change, returning to school and gaining the skills to build her own (now hugely successful) business. At the time, she said she was so mad at her boss, she couldn't imagine thanking him for anything. Here she was a single parent trying to provide for her children, and he was firing her because she didn't seem happy at work. And the truth was, she hadn't been happy.

To clear out her anger and step into her new direction, she wrote her boss a thank you letter. She thanked him for the gift he had given her saying that by firing her he helped her find the courage to go back to school and follow a dream she had delayed for many years. Later, she realized that accessing her gratitude and writing that letter were a turning point in her success.

Unknowingly, she had actually reprogrammed her brain to believe that negative experiences can bring positive results. Which of your past experiences can you point to that ultimately put you in a better position? Would you rather be bitter or better? Focus on how you became better from what came your way, and you can rewire your brain too.

This is the true nature of change. It happens to everyone, and if you were lucky enough to pay it forward with style and grace, you may reap the benefits of your good intentions.

The hand of change can sweep in at any moment. How you respond to someone else's change can be just as varied as how they choose to make their change. Some people change slowly, while you call from the sidelines, "Hurry up!' Others change on a dime. "I'm leaving, I've discovered my love for hunting lodges. See you at the end of the summer." "Uh, okay," you stammer, wishing you could go too. But no, this time they are going alone. Meanwhile you panic and feel terror—and if you're paying attention, you use the techniques we've practiced to calm yourself down. You focus on the positive: you're grateful that now you have the summer free and *voilà*, you move from the "reactor" role to that of "initiator." It is all about staying curious and then being proactive.

Stay flexible and ask yourself, "What does this bring up for me? How might I need to change here too?" Tone down the anxiety and tune up the curiosity to identify what's in it for you. When my parents died, I learned about an entirely different level of life. My father had Parkinson's disease, a terribly debilitating condition, and my mother cared for him for many years until she finally couldn't do it any longer. She was diagnosed with an aggressive form of cancer and died a short time later. My father lived a couple more years until he transitioned as well. Later I dreamed about them. In one dream, I was back in our family home where my father was bedridden and my mother was caring for him. In the dream, my mother was fast asleep on a rug in the bathroom and she appeared completely exhausted. I walked into my father's bedroom and said, "Dad, you do know that you're not sick anymore, right? You've died, you have moved on from this life." He turned to me and said, "Well I'm still a little sick, and so your mother is here taking care of me." When I woke up I wondered, had I not moved on either? What part of me was still sick over the loss of my parents, and how might I work it through to step more fully into the next phase of adulthood?

Resolution and evolution are a continuous process. Re-examine where and how you might need a change. Shake the hand of change so that it can leverage you into the new and unknown parts of yourself that need exploring.

ASK FOR HELP

I recently met a woman who studied a religion based on the idea that you can cure yourself through prayer. While some of what she said made sense to me, I couldn't figure out how you'd ever justify not getting a broken bone set when your child fell out of a tree. So I asked her about it. She explained that with something dramatic like a broken bone she would go to a doctor for help. And although her religion was based on the belief that the power to heal was received only through her connection with God, she had recently had a change of heart.

Several years ago she faced a health crisis that she initially tried to heal through faith and prayer. Her health did not improve, and finally her children intervened. They feared she had a life-threatening illness and reminded her that if she didn't get some help, she might not be around to see her grandchildren grow up. She said, "I realized I was going to have to humble myself and ask for help from another source." She explained how hard it was for her, that her community didn't support her decision to consult a medical doctor. Finally she kept her own counsel and went to the doctor who quickly diagnosed, and treated, her problem. Her children were relieved and thankful. She told me she felt this was a turning point in her life, as she realized that when you've done all you can do yourself, sometimes you simply need to reach out to others for help.

The same is true when creating change in your own life. While you are busy evolving, inevitably something in your Snapshot map will completely rock your world. At this point you either shrink or grow. Growth may be learning to ask for help when you need it. If you do not reach out to others, you risk losing an opportunity to keep your momentum going. The willpower and stamina you need to work on all your Bold Steps and reach your goals requires an immense amount of energy. At some point, you will need to reach out to others for help, support and encouragement. As the woman who consulted a doctor learned, reaching out for help, support and encouragement is not a sign of weakness, but rather an admission that you are wise enough to draw on all available resources.

A colleague's daughter was born without sight in one eye. When she first heard the news about her daughter's condition, the woman wanted so desperately to help she offered to donate one of her own eyes. While this was not medically possible my colleague and her husband pursued every available solution, including taking their daughter from Seattle to Los Angeles to participate in a research project. My colleague's desire to give "whatever it takes" may sound extreme, but some people's willingness to help knows no bounds.

If you are someone who rarely asks for help, here are some tips to follow: First, get specific about the kind of help you need. Write it out. Then identify people or organizations that might have possible solutions or resources for you. There will always be someone in your circle of friends and colleagues who is a six degrees of separation person—who knows a lot of people and enjoys connecting them with each other. Once you find your source, let them know what you are looking for. Take them to lunch, lay out your scenario, and then ask for help. Be ready to describe your quest in positive terms; no one wants to hear a litany of your failures and difficulties. Even if this doesn't immediately lead to a solution, you have signaled your intention to be open to solutions and the energy will be moving in the right direction.

Sometimes the help you need only becomes available when you surrender to the universe. If your standard way of operating is to micro-manage every detail and leave nothing to chance, this concept might sound very foreign to you. This is one of those times when you need to take a leap of faith and surrender to forces greater and wiser than yourself.

One of my drama therapy colleagues is a brilliant therapist. He can take the most unruly bunch of hooligans and, using drama techniques, transform them into a unified, playful, loving, supportive group of kids. When asked how he does it, he says that before every group session, he gets down on his knees and asks for strength and wisdom. He knows he doesn't have all the answers and can't do it alone, but surrendering his ego enables him to tap into universal force. I believe that's what makes his work so beautiful and profound.

Change takes courage and a ton of humility. It isn't easy to ask friends and colleagues to put in a good word for you with the hiring committee. Pride can get in your way. Your willingness to admit that you need others is an important step toward getting what you want.

HELP OTHERS

At this very moment, someone around you is panic-stricken over the change they are experiencing. If you scan your environment, I'll bet you know someone who realized that they were ready for a career change, started taking small steps toward making it happen, and then boom! Everything began to change, their regular source of income dried up and despite their best efforts, nothing was working. Or maybe you have a friend in the throes of parenting a strong-willed, typical teenager. They've just issued an ultimatum: do your homework or find your own place to live. And now they are wondering if they've done the right thing. Whatever the story, they are telling it to you and for the moment, you are their lifeline to sanity.

This is your chance to be the kind of support you want to have for yourself. Stop whatever you are doing and give them your full attention. Ask them to meet you for coffee, write a note to let them know you are thinking of them or send a funny card to make them laugh. Your gesture, big or small, will go a long way when someone is struggling. Ask if there is anything you can do for them (take them at their word if they say "nothing"), and be prepared to listen and provide encouragement.

Remember the series of sessions I conducted for the company that had just made some drastic staff cuts? The remaining employees were some of the angriest people I'd ever worked with. I was surprised at the deep, deep feelings of betrayal they expressed. Keeping the process moving and giving everyone a voice took every ounce of my skill as a facilitator, and I went home each night totally drained. About a week into the project, I came in one morning to find a card and a lovely pink glass heart on my desk.

The card was from the head of human resources and it read, "Thank you for your transparency and love during this process." The tiny heart, and her acknowledgement of what I was dealing with carried me through to the end of the sessions. Today I still keep the pink heart on my desk. Whenever I look at it I am reminded not to take things personally, to be transparent and open, and to remain curious about the process. It also helps me remember how important it is to make my own gestures of gratitude when I see someone who is carrying a heavy load.

Whatever tools, techniques and toys are in your resiliency toolbox, the most useful one is the ability to be honest with yourself and others about what a change is really going to mean.

In my work with individuals and companies around the world, I always say, "Be honest. Do not lie about the changes that are occurring. Sometimes telling the truth can feel like pulling the bandage off a wound, but keep in mind that if you know what is happening and do it quickly, it will be over sooner and the healing can begin."

Reflect on the people around you right now who are having a hard time, and find a way to reach out and be a source of support and encouragement for them. I guarantee your efforts will come back to you many times over.

FINAL THOUGHTS

Everything you ever wanted to become or experience is one visualization away. The mere act of visualizing and drawing your life and what you want will surprise you with its simplicity and power. In this book, I have introduced you to a simple process to help you set goals, and use visual imagery and other techniques to help you sustain your momentum. Along with recognizing the many things you already know about creating meaningful change, I hope you have learned new ideas and new ways of thinking about your life. My wish for you is that through working with this book, you have experienced a shift.

No matter what you are trying to accomplish, practice makes perfect—and so it is for the process of creating a life you love. You will need to develop new and different ways to stay inspired and engaged as your world evolves into your Desired New Reality.

Did you know that when engineers measured the foundation of the Egyptian pyramids against a computer model (if they were designing the pyramids today), the comparison was off by only 2 inches? When I read this, I was amazed. How on earth did the original builders accomplish this—with no calculators or high-tech equipment?

They did it by building a huge moat around the area where they wanted to build the pyramid. They filled the moat with water so they had a reliable level reference. And so it is with you. By using the techniques described here, you will have your own reliable, water-filled moat to help you discern where to place the first stones of the foundation of your new life. In time, this solid foundation will help you build all the things you long for now. With this support you will be in a good position to be generous with your talents, your creativity and your vision. And in time your gifts will expand to allow you to make your much needed, unique contribution to the world.

As one of my early collaborators would whisper to me before I went on stage, "Be brave, little soldier!"

PART FOUR

A QUICK GUIDE TO MAPPING

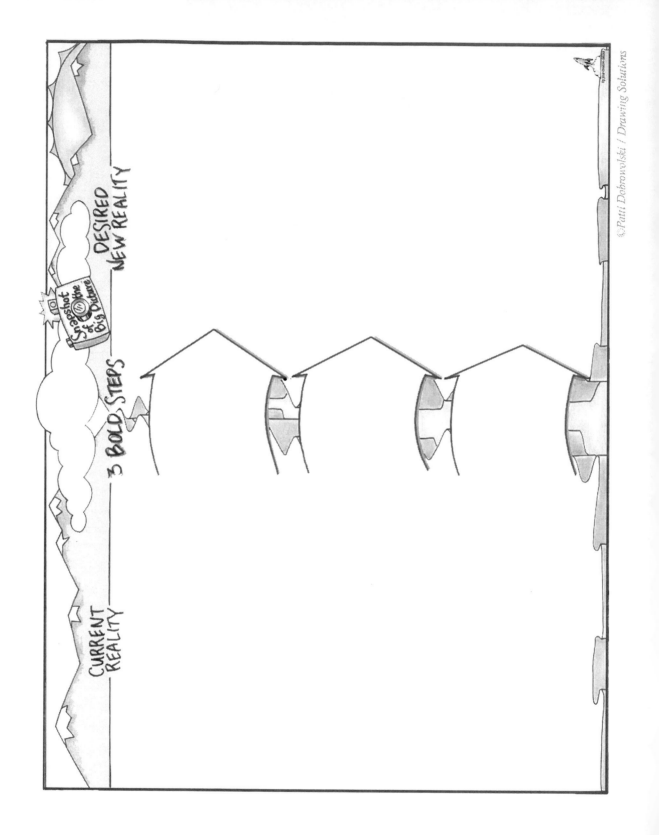

DESIRED
NEW REALITY

Snapshot of the Big Picture

CURRENT
REALITY

3 BOLD STEPS

QUICK GUIDE TO YOUR SNAPSHOT OF THE BIG PICTURE MAP OR MINI-MAP

(a Mini-Map focuses on one aspect of the larger picture of you)

Preparation

- •. Find a quiet place to work for about an hour where you will not be disturbed. Turn off all technological devices. Make a copy of the Snapshot of the Big Picture Map from the Appendix or download one from the website, www.upyourcreativegenius.com/snapshottemplate. Get some colored pencils, pens or crayons to work with.

- • Decide which part of your life you would like to focus on: work and career, relationship, friends or partnership, spirituality, a specific goal you want to accomplish, or your life as a whole.

Step 1: Name

Write your name in the cloud at the top center of the map. Color around it.

Step 2: Current Reality

What is the current state of you, your goal, your career, your _____?

- • Capture in words and images, on the left side of the map under "Current Reality," everything that comes to mind. Write and draw pictures of the things you are currently doing and how you think and feel about them. Capture the qualities and characteristics of what it is like to be you right now, or where you are in relationship to your goal. (For example, regarding your health: "Not exercising, good intentions, poor follow through." Career: "Project manager—no job—guilty (about not working)."

- Write legibly, and use the full space provided rather than "listing" things. Capture just the essence of the experience, not a full sentence.

- Color-code certain elements—brown or red for emotional or challenging areas, blue or light blue for current state elements/qualities of whatever you are.

- Add pictures to your words to activate both sides of your brain. THIS IS ESSENTIAL!

- Reflect on what you see, and add things that have been challenging for you. You might put them on a rock in the picture.

- Highlight things that feel like they have been a pattern for you.

Step Three: Desired New Reality

Take a break from what you are doing to change the pattern of your focus. Do something out of the ordinary—run around the house, play loud music, drink an eight-ounce glass of water, do some push-ups. Take some deep breaths. Then close your eyes to get centered. This also helps your brain sort the information for the next step. Then:

- Consciously remind the left side of your brain that it may not interfere in the next part of the process, that your intent is to be completely open and positive with what you discover in the process. When your critic emerges, banish it from the room.

- Ask yourself, "In the best-case scenario, one year from today, what will it be like to be me? What will it feel like to have accomplished this goal? What new things will I be experiencing in my love life? What qualities and characteristics will I be experiencing?"

- Capture the first things that come to mind, without censoring words and images, on the right side of the map under Desired New Reality.

- Color code it green, light green or a color representing growth or change for you.

- Reflect on what you have written and drawn. Add to the map anything you may have missed. If you have written anything with the word "no" attached to it, like "no stress," remove it and replace it with something positive, that indicates what you *would like* to be experiencing.

Step Four: 3 Bold Steps

Look at where you are now and where you want to be one year from today. Ask yourself, "What are the 3 boldest steps I can take to get myself from the left to the right side of the map? (A Bold Step is not rearranging your file cabinet, it is something that will challenge you on some level.)

- On a separate piece of paper, brainstorm without worrying about how bold of a step it is. Get as many ideas as you can. Once you have at least five, then choose your top three. The first is often very bold, the second may feel tactical, the third is often an emotional shift or internal process that you believe will get you where you want to be.

- Write them on the map in a different color—orange or red—something bright and optimistic.

Step Five: Action Steps

- Take each Bold Step and write it below.

- Under each Bold Step, make a list of 8-10 smaller actions you can take to achieve each of your bigger Bold Steps. For example:

Bold Step 1: *Quit my job*

Actions:

- *Tell my family I need to do something else and enlist their help*

- *Refresh my résumé*

- *Identify how much savings want to have before I give notice*

- Choose two of the 8-10 that will get you the biggest bang for your buck to put your energy behind them.

- Take action on these immediately. Transfer them into your "to do" list or calendar. Post your Snapshot map in a location where you can see it and dream about it often.

Bold Step 1:

Actions:

-
-
-

Bold Step 2:

Actions:

-
-
-

Bold Step 3:

Actions:

-
-
-

Step Six: Set Success Measures

Set simple success measures for each of your Bold Steps. When I have completed this Bold Step, what will success look like? What will I be doing as a result? How will I feel? What will people around me be saying?For example:

Bold Step One: *Quit My Job*

Success Measures:

- *My family is aware of and supports my decision*

- *My refreshed resume got me five interviews for the kind of work I want to be doing*

- *I have created a savings plan and made my first installment of $___ x ___*

Bold Step 1:

Success Measures:

-

-

-

Bold Step 2:

Success Measures:

-

-

-

Bold Step 3:

Success Measures:

-

-

-

Step Seven: Revisit and Reinvigorate Your Map Each Week

- When you accomplish a task, however small, celebrate immediately to reinforce continued progress. Say, "I drink this _____ in celebration of my continued success with _____."

- Set a time each week to revisit your map and your to-do list, and make a new list for the upcoming week. This might include transferring some things over to next week—however, if they remain for three weeks, discard them or break them down into smaller actions and choose something you can accomplish.

CHEAT SHEET IMAGES TO GET YOU STARTED

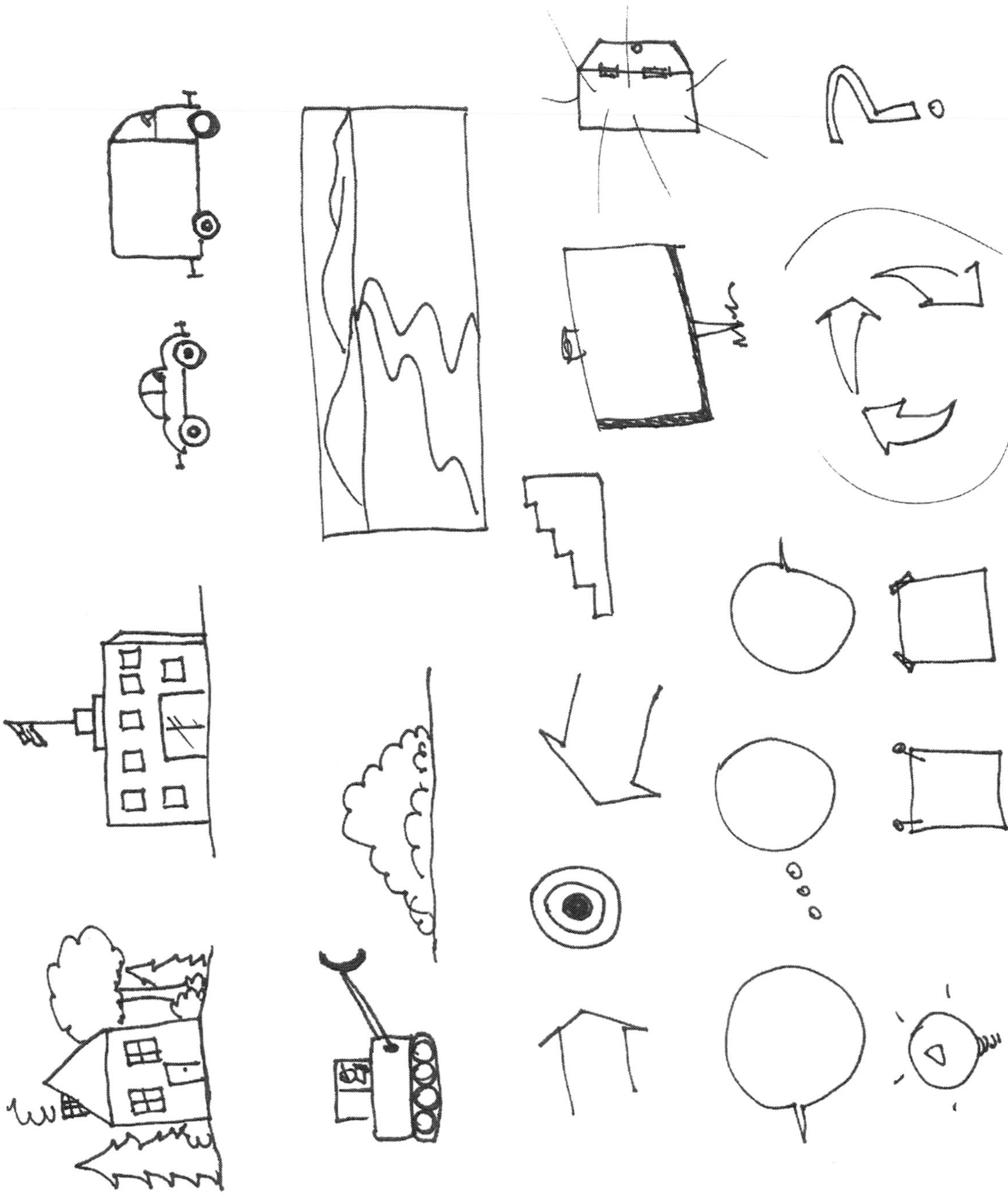

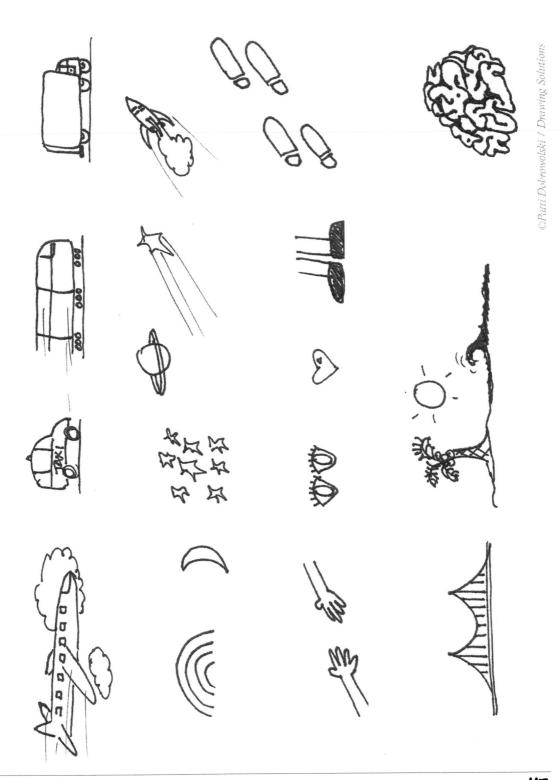

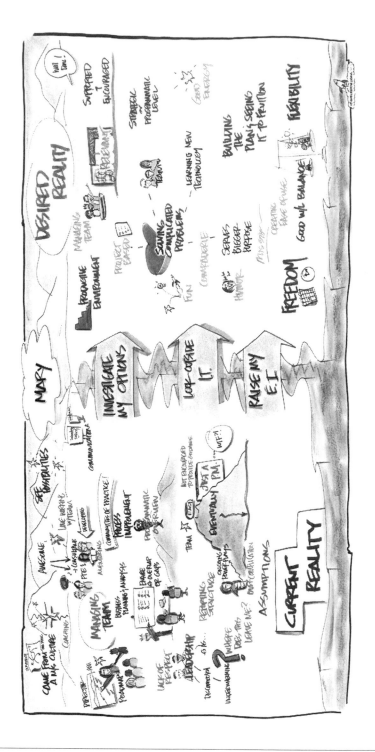

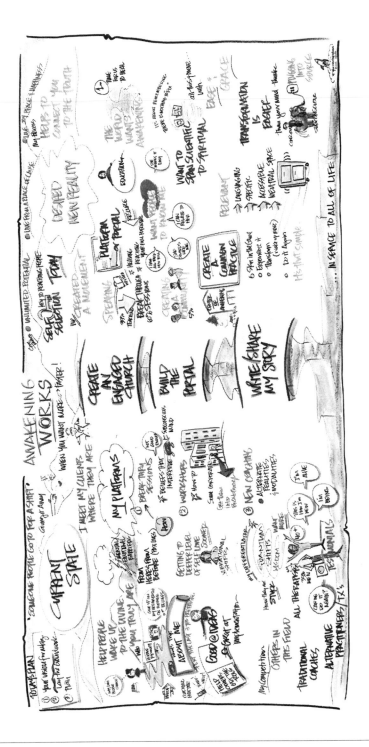

CURRENT STATE
MARK
DESIRED NEW REALITY
ALIGN WITH MY DESTINY
LEVERAGE MY CONNECTIONS
GET IN FRONT OF THE CAMERA
STICK
SELF WORTH
JOY
INTEGRATION & LEVERAGING OF EXPANDING TECHNOLOGY
MY JOB IS TO RECORD
FEEL FLOW
FRIENDSHIPS

APPENDIX

RESOURCES

Visual Processes

The Back of the Napkin, Dan Roam

Mapping Inner Space: Learning and Teaching Visual Mapping, Nancy Margulies and Nusa Maal

Strategic Vision Work, Ulric Rudebeck

Visual Meetings: How Graphics, Sticky Notes and Idea Mapping Can Transform Group Productivity, David Sibbet

Visual Thinking: Tools for Mapping Your Ideas, Nancy Margulies and Christine Valenza

Visual Processes Websites

International Forum of Visual Practitioners: www.ifvp.org/

Digital Roam: Visual thinking for the business world, www.digitalroam.com/

Tony Buzan: Mindmapping, www.thinkbuzan.com/uk

Brain Science

A Whole New Mind, Daniel Pink

Brain Rules, John Medina

The Secret Life of the Grown Up Brain, Barbara Strauch

Your Brain at Work, David Rock

Your Creative Brain, Seven Steps to Maximize Imagination, Productivity, and Innovation in Your Life, Shelley Carson, Ph.D.

Brain Science Websites

Neil F. Niemark, MD, www.thebodysoulconnection.com

Dan Pink, www.danpink.com

David Rock, blog.davidrock.net/

Dr. Ellen F. Weber, www.brainleadersandlearners.com

END NOTES

Section I

1. John Medina, *Brain Rules: 12 Principles for Surviving and Thriving at Work, Home, and School.* "The more visual the input becomes, the more likely it is to be recognized—and recalled." The phenomenon is so pervasive, it has been given its own name: the pictorial superiority effect, or PSE. — p. 233.

2. Pink, Daniel H. *A Whole New Mind: Why Right-Brainers Will Rule the Future.*

3. Roam, Dan. *The Back of the Napkin: Solving Problems and Selling Ideas with Pictures.*

4. Bruce Lipton, *The Biology of Belief: Unleashing the Power of Consciousness, Matter & Miracles.*

5. David Rock, *Your Brain at Work: Strategies for Overcoming Distraction, Regaining Focus, and Working Smarter All Day Long.*

6. Robert M. Williams, *Psyche-K: The Missing Peace in Your Life.*

7. Discovering the Virtues of a Wandering Mind," by John Tierney.

8. Dr. Eric Klinger, "Daydreaming and Fantasizing: Thought Flow and Motivation," in *Handbook of Imagination and Mental Stimulation*, Markman et al, Eds.

9. Bruce Lipton, *The Biology of Belief.*

10. Shelly Carlson, *Your Creative Brain: Seven Steps to Maximize Imagination, Productivity, and Innovation in Your Life.*

11. "The older you are, the more prone you are to being positive. Not because your brain wants to live out your life in a smiley stupor, but because researchers found that as you age, you focus on the more positive because you want to, it suits your goals." Barbara Straych, *The Secret Life of the Grown-up Brain.*

12. Dan Roam, *The Back of the Napkin.*

13. Alan Deutschman, *Change or Die: The Three Keys to Change at Work & in Life*.

14. John Medina, *Brain Rules*.

15. "Nurturing creativity is one of the most important things you can do for your child," says Wendy Masi, Ph.D, Dean of the Mailman Segal Institute of Childhood Studies at Nova Southeastern University, and author of *Toddler Play*. New research indicates that a child's Imagination Quotient (aka "the other IQ") may be a bigger factor in predicting academic success than the more traditional measure of aptitude.

16. Elisabeth Kübler-Ross, *The Wheel of Life: A Memoir of Living and Dying*.

17. "Biobehavioral Responses to Stress in Females: Tend-and-Befriend, Not Fight-or-Flight," *Psychological Review*, Vol. 107, No. 3, Shelley E. Taylor, Laura Cousino Klein, Brian P. Lewis, Tara L. Gruenewald, Regan A.R. Guryng, and John A. Updegraff

18. Bruce Lipton, *The Biology of Belief*.

Section II

1. There are two size options to download – one small file to print on 8 1/2 "x 11" paper, or a larger one that you can take to your local copy center and print in 11x17 format. You can also order a big one (4'x8') online **www.upyourcreativegenius.com/snapshottemplate** which will give you plenty of room to capture everything large in living color.

2. Cognitive Control in Media Multitaskers," *PNAS*, Vol. 106, No. 37. Eyal Ophir, Clifford Nass and Anthony D. Wagner found in a study that heavy multitaskers performed worse on a test of task-switching ability.

3. Betty Edwards, *The New Drawing on the Right Side of the Brain*.

4. Dian Buchman, Ph.D. *The Complete Book of Water Healing*.

5. David Rock, *Your Brain At Work*.

6. Steve Andreas and Charles Faulkner (Eds.), *NLP: The New Technology of Achievement*.

7. John Medina, *Brain Rules*.

8. Robert M. Williams, *Psyche-K … The Missing Peace in Your Life*.

9. The concept of "magnetizing" or attracting positive outcomes, popularized in books

and film as the "Law of Attraction," dates back to the New Thought movement of the early 1900s with William Walter Atkinson's *Thought Vibration or the Law of Attraction* (1906, reissued 2007).

10. Alan Cohen, "Carpe Diem!" from *Dare to Be Yourself.* In *Chicken Soup for the Soul*, by Jack Canfield and Mark Victor Hansen.

11. Finding True North is essential for accurate navigation, hence the metaphor. In life's journey we are often uncertain where we stand, where we are going and what is our right path. Knowing our True North helps us follow the right path.

Section III

1. Bruce Lipton, *The Biology of Belief.*

2. Neil F. Neimark, M.D. at www.thebodysoulconnection.com/EducationCenter/fight.html

3. Bruce Bower, "The Write Stuff for Test Anxiety," *Science News.*

4. Eckhart Tolle, *A New Earth: Awakening to Your Life's Purpose.*

5. David Rock, *Your Brain at Work*, page 113.

6. The process of assessing where you are now, identifying what you desire in the future and creating steps for getting there by using images enhances the brain's ability to produce neurochemicals that make us feel excited. It actually creates a state of euphoria.

7. Dennis T. Jaffe and Cynthia D. Scott, *Managing Organisational Change.*

8. David Rock, *Your Brain at Work*, page 129.

9. David Rock, *Your Brain at Work.*

BIBLIOGRAPHY

Andreas, Steve, and Charles Faulkner (Eds). *NLP: The New Technology of Achievement.* New York, NY:Quill/William Morrow. 1994.

Bower, Bruce, "The Write Stuff for Test Anxiety," *Science News*, February 12, 2011, Vol.179 No. 4, pg. 9.

Brizendine, Louann, M.D. *The Female Brain*. New York, NY: Broadway Books. 2006.

Buchman, Dian Dincin. *The Complete Book of Water Healing: Using Earth's Most Essential Resource to Cure Illness, Promote Health, and Soothe and Restore Body, Mind and Spirit.* Chicago, IL: Contemporary Books. 2002

Canfield, Jack, and Mark Victor Hansen. *Chicken Soup for the Soul.* Deerfield Beach, FL: Health Communications, Inc. 1993.

Carson, Shelley, Ph.D. *Your Creative Brain: Seven Steps to Maximize Imagination, Productivity, and Innovation in Your Life.* San Francisco, CA: JosseyBass. 2010.

Cohen, Alan. *Dare to Be Yourself.* Des Moines, WA: Alan Cohen Publications. 1991.

Crowley, Chris, and Henry S. Lodge, M.D. *Younger Next Year for Women: Live Strong, Fit, and Sexy—Until You're 80 and Beyond.* New York, NY: Workman Publishing. 2007.

DePorter, Bobbi, with Mike Hernacki. *Quantum Learning: Unleashing the Genius in You.* New York, NY: Dell Publishing. 1992.

Deutschman, Alan. *Change or Die: The Three Keys to Change at Work and in Life.* New York, NY: HarperCollins. 2007.

Doidge, Norman, M.D. *The Brain That Changes Itself: Stories of Personal Triumph from the Frontiers of Brain Science.* New York, NY: Penguin Group. 2007.

Dylan, Peggy, and Tolly Burkan. *Guiding Yourself Into a Spiritual Reality: 25-Year Anniversary Edition.* Sonora, CA: New Voices, Inc. 2009

Edwards, Betty. *The New Drawing on the Right Side of the Brain*. New York, NY : Jeremy P. Tarcher/Putnam. 1999.

Godin, Seth. *Poke the Box: When Was the Last Time You Did Something for the First Time?* Amazon: Do You Zoom Inc. 2011.

Heath, Chip, and Dan Heath. *Switch: How to Change Things When Change Is Hard*. New York, NY: Broadway Books. 2010.

Jaffe, Dennis T. and Cynthia D. Scott. *Managing Organisational Change*. London, U.K.: Kogan Page Ltd. 1990.

Kübler-Ross, Elisabeth. *The Wheel of Life: A Memoir of Living and Dying*. New York, NY: Touchstone Books. 1997

Lipton, Bruce H., Ph.D. *The Biology of Belief: Unleashing the Power of Consciousness, Matter & Miracles*. Carlsbad, CA: Hay House. 2008.

Margulies, Nancy, and Nusa Maal. *Mapping Inner Space: Learning and Teaching Visual Mapping*. Tucson, AZ: Zephyr Press. 2002.

Margulies, Nancy, and Christine Valenza. *Visual Thinking: Tools for Mapping Your Ideas*. Norwalk, CT: Crown House Publishing Co. 2005.

Markman, Keith D., William M. P. Klein and Julie A. Suhr (Eds.). *Handbook of Imagination and Mental Stimulation*. New York, NY: Psychology Press. 2009

Masi, Wendy S., Ph.D. *Toddler Play*. San Francisco, CA: Creative Publishing International. 2001.

McWilliams, Peter. *You Can't Afford the Luxury of A Negative Thought*. Los Angeles, CA: Prelude Press. 1995.

Medina, John J. *Brain Rules: 12 Principles for Surviving and Thriving at Work, Home, and School*. Seattle, WA: Pear Press. 2008.

Moore, Mary Carroll. *How to Master Change in Your Life: 67 Ways to Handle Life's Toughest Moments*. Chanhassen, MN: Eckankar. 2010.

Ophir, Eyal, Clifford Nass, and Anthony D. Wagner. "Cognitive Control in Media Multitaskers." *The Proceedings of the National Academy of Sciences*. September 15, 2009: Vol. 106, No. 37, pp. 15583-15587.

Pink, Daniel H. *A Whole New Mind: Why Right-Brainers Will Rule the Future*. New York, NY: Riverhead Books. 2005.

_____. *Drive: The Surprising Truth About What Motivates Us*. New York, NY: Riverhead Books. 2009.

Roam, Dan. *The Back of the Napkin: Solving Problems and Selling Ideas with Pictures*. New York, NY: Penguin Group. 2008.

Rock, David. *Your Brain at Work: Strategies for Overcoming Distraction, Regaining Focus, and Working Smarter All Day Long*. New York, NY: HarperCollins. 2009.

Rudebeck, Ulric. *Strategic Vision Work: Create an Organisation that Works for You*. Stockholm, Sweden: Urvision. 2008.

Sibbet, David. *Visual Meetings: How Graphics, Sticky Notes & Idea Mapping Can Transform Group Productivity*. Hoboken, NJ: John Wiley & Sons. 2010.

Strauch, Barbara. *The Secret Life of the Grown-up Brain: The Surprising Talents of the Middle-Aged Mind*. New York, NY: Penguin Group. 2010.

Taylor, Shelley E., Laura Coysino Klein, Brian P. Lewis, Tara L. Gruenewald, Regan A.R. Guryng, and John A. Updegraff. "Biobehavioral Responses to Stress in Females: Tend-and-Befriend, Not Flight-or-Fright." *Psychological Review*. 2000: Vol. 107, No. 3, pp. 411-429.

Tierney, John. "Discovering the Virtues of a Wandering Mind," *The New York Times*, June 28, 2010.

Tolle, Eckhart. *A New Earth: Awakening to Your Life's Purpose*. New York, NY: Penguin Group. 2005.

Williams, Robert M. *Psych-K ... The Missing Peace in Your Life*. Crestone, CO: Myrddin Publications. 2004.

Zander, Rosamund Stone and Benjamin Zander. *The Art of Possibility: Transforming Professional and Personal Life*. New York, NY: Penguin Books, 2000.

ACKNOWLEDGMENTS

This book is dedicated to those of you I met on planes, in meetings, at grocery stores, bike races, or in any queue where we were waiting long enough for you to share with me your stories of navigating change. Those stories inspired me and helped shape this book. I extend a special thanks to those people who challenged my skills and thinking: Dr. Jonathon Rosenfeld and Dr. Adria Blum, my psychology collaborators; Michael Stark, for many fantastic years of encouragement and coaching; Janet Schatzman and Kevin Woodson who taught me to illustrate boldly and with intention; John Tedstrom from Hawkeye for his unparalleled enthusiasm and creativity; and Suzanne Simmons, Martin Matthews, Alan Krepack and the team at Changeworks Global for giving me a good kick start. Thanks to Tom Bird and Paul McCarthy who offered great guidance during early versions of the manuscript. Unparalleled editing was contributed by Patricia Kyritsi Howell, expert line editing by Christin Whittington and Karen Bentley; special thanks to Jamie Saloff who put it all in its rightful place.

Thank you to my clients for inspiration and their support for me and my work: Barbara Beasley at McKesson; Dean Capon, Sheila Broadley, Jacqui Spencer, the senior team and Dan Zabrowski at Hoffman-LaRoche; Wim Lammertink at Pall Corporation; Lily Ruppe; Scott Simmons at Johns Manville; Maria Berardo, Lucy Hur and John Williams at Microsoft; Pam Austin and Norma Miller at The Bill & Melinda Gates Foundation; and the leadership team at Tastefully Simple. To the other graphic recorders who helped to shape my images and beliefs: Nancy Margulies, Kriss Wittmann, Janine Underhill, Julie Primozich, Tim Corey, Nancy White, Keith McCandless and Stephen Right.

I have been fortunate to have the support of a strong circle of friends and family. I thank them for being there for me through my own transitions: Molly Thompson and Joe Casalini, Julia Thompson and Ray McFarland, Kevin and Sooz Duggan, Brad Clemmons and Pamela Harris, Patti Howell and Robinette Kennedy, Dawn Pinaud, Mike Schwartz and my comic collaborator Nancy Cranbourne, and my super creative soul mate, Scott Ward. Special thanks to Chris Chopyak and Lois Todd, my former business partners at Alchemy: The Art of Transforming Business who helped me find my voice, supported my own need for change and taught me about kindness. My spiritual family, Frank Martorelli, Beth Berger and Karen Candito (who braved early drafts of this book) contributed to the creation of this manuscript by helping keep me on track.

To my family and champions: Jim, Jan, Jessica, and Jon Dobrowolski, Joan, Olek and Aleks Urbaniak, Carol and Jeff Brown and Jake Augustine, I extend my heartfelt thanks for your encouragement, sense of humor and the wisdom you have shared with me.

Finally, I am thankful for the love and support of my wonderful and brilliant partner, Julie Boardman, who kept me believing I would make it to the end! For your constant love and encouragement, ideation skills, strategic mindset, and utmost patience, thank you, thank you, *thank you*!

ABOUT THE AUTHOR

Patti Dobrowolski is the founder of Up Your Creative Genius, a consulting firm that uses visuals and creative processes to help companies and individuals around the world accelerate growth and change. A critically acclaimed comic performer, internationally recognized keynote speaker, writer and business consultant, she has been the recipient of numerous business awards including the *Make Mine A Million $ Business* program. She has brought her innovative visual practices to Microsoft Corporation, The Bill & Melinda Gates Foundation, Pall Corporation, Johns Manville, Hoffman-LaRoche Pharmaceuticals, McKesson, Gilead Sciences, USDA, Intermec Technologies, FedEx, Starbucks, Pepsico, and multiple universities across the United States.

Known for her high energy, quick wit and commitment to helping people and businesses achieve their goals, she lives in the rainforest of Seattle, Washington with her partner Julie, 3 dogs and 3 chickens.

CPSIA information can be obtained at www.ICGtesting.com
Printed in the USA
BVOW060142090513

320267BV00003B/5/P